Oriental Encounters

ORIENTAL ENCOUNTERS

PALESTINE AND SYRIA 1894 - 96

By MARMADUKE PICKTHALL

ONESUCH PRESS

LONDON   MELBOURNE   NASHVILLE

Onesuch Press enriches lives by reclaiming the forgotten past; publishing the lesser known works of great writers and the great works of forgotten ones. For more information about us visit www.onesuchpress.com.

A ONESUCH BOOK
Published by ONESUCH PRESS
PO Box 303BK, Black Hill 3350 Australia

The first edition of *Oriental Encounters* was published in 1918. This edition, first published in 2012 is based on that text. It has been reset with minor emendations.

National Library of Australia Cataloguing-in-Publication entry
Author: Pickthall, Muhammad Marmaduke, 1875 - 1936.
Title: Oriental Encounters : Palestine and Syria (1894-6)
Marmaduke Pickthall

ISBN: 978 0 9871532-6-5 (pbk.)
ISBN: 978 0 9872760-9-4 (ebook)

Subjects: Pickthall, Muhammad Marmaduke, 1875 - 1936. – Travel
Palestine–Description and travel–19th century.
Syria–Description and travel–19th century.

Dewey Number: 956.94

The paper used in this publication meets the minimum requirements of ANSI/NISO Z39.48-1992 (R1997) (Permanence of Paper). The paper used in this book is from responsibly managed forests. Printed in the United States of America, the United Kingdom and Australia by Lightning Source, Inc.

Contents

ABOUT THE AUTHOR	VII
PUBLISHER'S NOTE	XV
INTRODUCTION	XVII
RASHÎD THE FAIR	1
A MOUNTAIN GARRISON	7
THE RHINOCEROS WHIP	12
THE COURTEOUS JUDGE	17
NAWÂDIR	23
POLICE WORK	44
MY COUNTRYMAN	50
THE PARTING OF THE WAYS	56
THE KNIGHT ERRANT	62
THE FANATIC	69
RASHÎD'S REVENGE	74
THE HANGING DOG	80
TIGERS	85
PRIDE AND A FALL	91
TRAGEDY	97
BASTIRMA	103
THE ARTIST-DRAGOMAN	109
LOVE AND THE PATRIARCH	114
THE UNPOPULAR LANDOWNER	121
THE CAÏMMACÂM	128
CONCERNING BRIBES	134
THE BATTLEFIELD	139
MURDERERS	146
THE TREES ON THE LAND	151
BUYING A HOUSE	158
A DISAPPOINTMENT	164
CONCERNING CRIME & PUNISHMENT	170
THE UNWALLED VINEYARD	176
THE ATHEIST	182
THE SELLING OF OUR GUN	189
MY BENEFACTOR	195

Marmaduke Pickthall is well known to millions of readers for his translation *The Meaning of the Glorious Qur'ân* (1930), considered his crowning achievement. It is the first translation by a Muslim whose native language was English. He believed that the Qur'an could never be perfectly translated out of Arabic, but his work contains the most beautiful and rich use of English, similar in many ways to the prose poetry of Tyndale's Bible.

He was born in 1875 in Suffolk and at age five, on the death of his father, moved to London. As a child he suffered from bronchitis and meningitis which affected his growing interest in arithmetic. As a boy, painfully shy, he spent six unhappy terms at Harrow where he befriended Winston Churchill.

He then travelled throughout Europe with his mother, discovering and perfecting a talent for language. In the Jura Mountains he acquired a love of mountaineering, and in Wales and Ireland he learned Welsh and Gaelic. Marmaduke sat for exams to enter the Levant Consular Service, but despite outstanding marks in language, he placed too low in the other areas. His choices were to either return to Harrow and continue on to Oxford, or take up the invitation of Thomas Dowling, a friend of his mother's, who was going to Palestine to serve as chaplain to the Anglican Bishop of Jerusalem.

Before leaving he proposed to his future wife, Muriel Smith. She accepted but lost her betrothed to the East for several years.

Hoping to learn enough Arabic to earn him a consular job in Palestine, Marmaduke at seventeen, sailed for Port Said. He spent weeks wandering Cairo, developing an empathy for the poorer inhabitants. He found a *khoja* to teach him Arabic, and with increasing fluency, took ship for Jaffa where to the horror of the Europeans he donned native garb and disappeared into the Palestinian hinterland.

Later in life he wrote: *When I read The Arabian Nights I see the daily life of Damascus, Jerusalem, Aleppo, Cairo, and the other cities as I found it in the early nineties of last century. What struck me, even in its decay and poverty, was the joyousness of that life compared with anything that I had seen in Europe. The people seemed quite independent of our cares of life, our anxious clutching after wealth, our fear of death.'*

He wrote some of these experiences in *Oriental Encounters*. He had found an exotic world of intoxicating freedom unimaginable to a public schoolboy raised in structured, regulated England. Most Palestinians never set eyes on a policeman, and lived for decades without engaging with government in any way. Islamic law was administered in its time-honoured fashion, by *Qadis* who for the most part were local scholars. Villages chose their own headmen, or inherited them, and the same was true for the Bedouin tribes.

He would have converted to Islam there but for his Muslim teacher, the *Sheykh-ul-Ulema* of the great mosque at Damascus. Marmaduke mentioned his desire to become a Muslim but the *Sheykh* reminded him of his duty to his mother and forbade him to profess Islam until he had consulted her. *'No, my son,'* were his words, *'wait until you are older, and have seen again your native land. You are alone among us as our boys are alone among the Christians. God knows how I should feel if any Christian teacher dealt with a son of mine otherwise than as I now deal with you.'*

In 1896, reports of his having 'gone native' reached his mother and the twenty-year-old Marmaduke was called home.

Back in London he married Muriel in September 1896 then spirited her to Geneva, partly for the skiing but also to associate with the literary circles which he admired. He worked on the skills which would make him one of the most distinguished exponents both of novel-writing and of the fledgling sport of skiing. In 1898 he published his first short story. His first Near Eastern story, the intense *The Word of an Englishman*, was also published the same year. By 1899, the financially-strapped couple took a small cottage in Suffolk where Marmaduke could write on a regular basis.

His first novel, *All Fools* was published in 1900. It contained passages that for the time, crossed a moral line and embarrassed his mother with its references to unmentionable items of Victorian underwear. Even the Anglican Bishop of Jerusalem expressed concerns, so after his second novel *Saïd the Fisherman* was published in 1902, Marmaduke bought up and destroyed the remaining copies of *All Fools*.

By 1903 fan-mail began to arrive at the cottage in Suffolk. One letter came from H.G. Wells, who wrote, *'I wish that I could feel as certain about my own work as I do of yours, that it will be alive and interesting people fifty years from now.'*

For the next few years, Marmaduke published a novel a year, including *Enid, Brendle*, and *The House of Islam*. In 1907 an invitation to St James's Palace to meet the wife of Captain Machell, advisor to the Egyptian Prime Minister Mustafa Fahmi Pasha, began with a discussion of his books, and led to an invitation to Alexandria. Ten years after his first departure he was back in his beloved East. In native dress again, he travelled through the countryside.

But the old Ottoman Empire had declined in the face of expansion by the Austro-Hungarian Empire on the one hand and Russia on the other. By 1908 intimations of the collapse were clear. At first, the Young Turk revolution seemed a time of hope for the Empire. Marmaduke hoped the revolutionaries would hold the empire together better than the old Sultan with his secretive ways. In 1912 the Empire lost her remaining European territories to vengeful Christians in the disaster that was the Balkan War. The new Sultan refused to allow the Balkan Muslims to retain their arms and the results were the religious pogroms of 1912 and 1913.

Back in England, Marmaduke campaigned on Turkey's behalf, but could do nothing against the new Foreign Secretary who was *'Russophile, Germanophobe, and anti-Islamic.'* Marmaduke wrote to the Foreign Office demanding to know whether the new arrangements in the Balkans could be considered to further the cause of peace, and received this reply: *'Yes, and I'll tell you why. It is not generally known. But the Muslim population has been practically wiped out—* 240,000 *killed in Western Thrace alone—that clears the ground.'*

In 1913 Lady Evelyn Cobbold, heiress and traveller, offered to convert him to Islam during a dinner at Claridges. At the time he demurred. But by the following year the sanctimony of the church repelled him. In a small Sussex village church Marmaduke listened to the vicar reviling the devilish Turk. He thought of the forced conversions of the Pomaks in Bulgaria and the atrocities committed by Christian soldiers removing the lips of refugees in Istanbul for trophies. He could stand no more and left the church before the end of the service. He never again considered himself a Christian.

In 1915 the Turks trounced the British and colonial troops at Gallipoli, only to be betrayed by the Arab uprising under

Lawrence. Marmaduke despised Lawrence as a shallow romantic given to unnatural passions and wild misjudgements. As he later wrote, reviewing the Seven Pillars of Wisdom:

'He really thought the Arabs a more virile people than the Turks. He really thought them better qualified to govern. He really believed that the British Government would fulfil punctually all the promises made on its behalf. He really thought that it was love of freedom and his personal effort and example rather than the huge sums paid by the British authorities and the idea of looting Damascus, which made the Arabs zealous in rebellion.'

Throughout the Great War he wrote extensively in support of the Ottomans. When a vicious propaganda campaign was launched in 1915 over the massacres of Armenians, Marmaduke, showing courage and integrity, argued that all the blame could not be placed on the Turkish government. Even so, he was ready to fight for his country as long as he did not have to fight the Turks. He was conscripted in the last months of the war and became corporal in charge of an influenza isolation hospital. The Foreign Office would have used his talents as a linguist but regarded him as a security risk

In 1918 Marmaduke announced his conversion to Islam and Muriel followed him soon after. He began to take up the reigns of leadership in the small British community of Muslims. There was a prayer-room in Notting Hill, an Islam Society and a Muslim Literary Society. Finally he assumed the Friday prayers at the Anglo-Moghul mosque in Woking

By then Britain had promised Istanbul and the Turkish-speaking areas of Thrace to post-war Turkey; but the reality turned out differently. Istanbul was placed under Allied occupation, and the bulk of Muslim Thrace was awarded to Greece. This turnabout intensified Indian Muslim mistrust of British rule. Gandhi too, called Hindus to the Khilafat movement supporting the Ottomans.

Marmaduke, now in direct opposition to his former friend Churchill, was outspoken against British policy. *'Objectivity is much more common in the East than in the West; nations, like individuals, are there judged by their words, not by their own idea of their intentions or beliefs; and these inconsistencies, which no doubt look very trifling to a British politician, impress the Oriental as a foul injustice and the outcome of fanaticism. The East preserves our record, and reviews it as a whole. There is no end visible to the absurdities into which this mental deficiency of our rulers may lead us.'*

The end of the War ushered in the next stage of his life. He accepted an invitation to be the editor of a great Indian newspaper, the Bombay Chronicle. By September 1919 he was deeply immersed in Indian life and politics. Within six months he had doubled the paper's circulation with its advocacy for Indian independence. The furious Government could do little.

Marmaduke developed a close association with Gandhi and supported the rejection of violent resistance to British rule. He refashioned himself into an Indian nationalist leader, fluent in Urdu, attending dawn prayers in the mosque in homespun clothes. He wrote to a friend: *They expect me to be a sort of political leader as well as a newspaper editor. I have grown quite used to haranguing multitudes of anything from 5 to 30,000 people in the open air, although I hate it still as much as ever and inwardly am just as miserably shy.'* He also continued his Friday sermons, preaching at the great mosque of Bijapur and elsewhere.

In 1924 the Raj imposed crippling fines on the paper for misreporting and Marmaduke resigned. He effectively left political life but was always remembered kindly by Gandhi, who was later to write to his widow: *Your husband and I met often enough to grow to love each other and I found Mr. Pickthall a most amiable and deeply religious man. And although he was a convert he had nothing of the fanatic in him that most converts, no matter to what faith they are converted, betray in their speech and act. Mr. Pickthall seemed to me to live his faith unobtrusively.'*

Marmaduke accepted the headmastership of a boy's school in the domain of the Nizam of Hyderabad, outside the authority of British India. In the 1920s Hyderabad resembled a surviving fragment of Moghul brilliance, and the Nizam, the richest man in the world, was turning his capital into an oasis of culture and art. The appointment of the celebrated Pickthall would add a further jewel to his crown. Marmaduke's monarchist sympathies were aroused by the Nizam, who had made his lands the pride of India. *'He lives like a dervish',* Marmaduke reported, *'and devotes his time to every detail of the Government.'*

During this time he wrote a Moghul novel *Dust and the Peacock Throne* which has never been published. Between 1929 and 1931 the Nizam gave him leave-of-absence to complete his Qur'ânic translation. He was anxious that this should be the most accurate, as well as the most literate, version of the Scripture. As well as mastering the classical Islamic sources, he travelled to Germany to consult with leading Orientalists.

When the translation was finished Marmaduke travelled to Egypt to have the work approved by the *Ulema* at Al-Azhar. He was disappointed to find that powerful factions deemed any translation of the Qur'ân was unlawful. One *Sheykh* went so far as to proclaim that all involved in such a project would burn in Hell for eternity.

Marmaduke wrote *'Many Egyptian Muslims were as surprised as I was at the extraordinary ignorance of present world conditions of men who claimed to be the thinking heads of the Islamic world – men who think that the Arabs are still 'the patrons,' and the non-Arabs their 'freedmen'; who cannot see that the positions have become reversed, that the Arabs are no longer the fighters and the non-Arabs the stay-at-homes but it is the non-Arabs who at present bear the brunt of the Jihâd; that the problems of the non-Arabs are not identical with those of the Arabs; that translation of the Qur'ân is for the non-Arabs a necessity, which, of course, it is not for Arabs; men who cannot conceive that there are Muslims in India as learned and devout, as capable as judgment and as careful for the safety of Islam, as any to be found in Egypt.'*

Marmaduke prevailed however when he debated in Arabic a large gathering of the Ulema. He explained the possibilities for the spread of Islam among the English-speaking people. The wiser of the al-Azhar, recognising their inability to understand the situation of English speakers accepted his translation.

It was published in 1930, and was hailed by the Times Literary Supplement as *'a great literary achievement.'* Unusually for a translation, it was further translated into several other languages, including Tagalog, Turkish and Portuguese.

Marmaduke was by now a revered religious leader. As such, he was asked by the Nizam to arrange the marriage of the heir to his throne to the daughter of the last Ottoman Caliph, Princess Dürrüsehvar. The Ottoman exiles lived in France as pensioners of the Nizam, and there Marmaduke and the Hyderabad contingent travelled. His knowledge of Ottoman and Moghul protocol allowed Pickthall to bring off this brilliant match.

In 1935 Marmaduke left Hyderabad, his flourishing school and handed over the reins of the journal Islamic Culture to a new editor to return to England.

He died in a cottage in the West Country in May 1936, of coronary thrombosis, and is buried in the Muslim cemetery at Brookwood.

The original text uses the archaic pronouns, thee, thou and thine along with corresponding verb conjugations (dost, shalt, wilt etc.) extensively. While this may convey in translation a certain formality present in Arabic speech, its effect overall on the narrative now seems awkward and dated. To make the book more readable we have replaced the archaic forms with modern ones, trusting that Pickthall, were he alive, might not have been too offended.

INTRODUCTION

Early in the year 1894 I was a candidate for one of two vacancies in the Consular Service for Turkey, Persia, and the Levant, but failed to gain the necessary place in the competitive examination. I was in despair. All my hopes for months had been turned towards sunny countries and old civilisations, away from the drab monotone of London fog, which seemed a nightmare when the prospect of escape eluded me. I was eighteen years old, and, having failed in one or two adventures, I thought myself an all-round failure, and was much depressed. I dreamed of Eastern sunshine, palm trees, camels, desert sand, as of a Paradise which I had lost by my shortcomings. What was my rapture when my mother one fine day suggested that it might be good for me to travel in the East, because my longing for it seemed to indicate a natural instinct, with which she herself, possessing Eastern memories, was in full sympathy!

I fancy there was some idea at the time that if I learnt the languages and studied life upon the spot I might eventually find some backstairs way into the service of the Foreign Office; but that idea, though cherished by my elders as some excuse for the expenses of my expedition, had never, from the first, appealed to me; and from the moment when I got to Egypt, my first destination, it lost whatever lustre it had had at home. For then the European ceased to interest me, appearing somehow inappropriate and false in those surroundings. At first I tried to overcome this feeling or perception which, while I lived with English people, seemed unlawful. All my education until then had tended to impose on me the cult of the thing done habitually upon a certain plane of our society. To seek to mix on an equality with Orientals, of whatever breeding, was one of those things which were never done, nor even contemplated, by the kind of person who had always been my model.

My sneaking wish to know the natives of the country intimately, like other unconventional desires I had at times experienced, might have remained a sneaking wish until this day, but for an accident which freed me for a time from English supervision. My people had provided me with introductions to several influential English residents in Syria, among others to a family of good position in Jerusalem; and it was understood that, on arrival in that country, I should go directly to that family for information and advice. But, as it chanced, on board the ship which took me to Port Said from Naples I met a man who knew those people intimately—had been, indeed, for years an inmate of their house—and he assumed the office of my mentor. I stayed in Cairo, merely because he did, for some weeks, and went with him on the same boat to Jaffa. He, for some unknown reason—I suspect insanity—did not want me in Jerusalem just then; and, when we landed, spun me a strange yarn of how the people I had thought to visit were exceedingly eccentric and uncertain in their moods; and how it would be best for me to stop in Jaffa until he sent me word that I was sure of welcome. His story was entirely false, I found out later, a libel on a very hospitable house. But I believed it at the time, as I did all his statements, having no other means of information on the subject.

So I remained at Jaffa, in a little gasthaus in the German colony, which had the charms of cleanliness and cheapness, and there I might have stayed till now had I awaited the tidings promised by my counsellor. There for the first two weeks I found life very dull. Then Mr. Hanauer, the

English chaplain, and a famous antiquarian, took pity on my solitary state, walked me about, and taught me words of Arabic. He was a native of Jerusalem, and loved the country. My sneaking wish to fraternise with Orientals, when I avowed it after hesitations, appeared good to him. And then I made acquaintance with a clever dragoman and one of the most famous jokers in all Syria, who happened to be lodging at my little hostelry, with nothing in the world to do but stare about him. He helped me to throw off the European and plunge into the native way of living. With him I rode about the plain of Sharon, sojourning among the fellâhîn, and sitting in the coffee-shops of Ramleh, Lydda, Gaza, meeting all sorts of people, and acquiring the vernacular without an effort, in the manner of amusement. From dawn to sunset we were in the saddle. We went on pilgrimage to Nebi Rubîn, the mosque upon the edge of marshes by the sea, half-way to Gaza; we rode up northward to the foot of Carmel; explored the gorges of the mountains of Judæa; frequented Turkish baths; ate native meals and slept in native houses—following the customs of the people of the land in all respects. And I was amazed at the immense relief I found in such a life. In all my previous years I had not seen happy people. These were happy. Poor they might be, but they had no dream of wealth; the very thought of competition was unknown to them, and rivalry was still a matter of the horse and spear. Wages and rent were troubles they had never heard of. Class distinctions, as we understand them, were not. Everybody talked to everybody. With inequality they had a true fraternity. People complained that they were badly governed, which merely meant that they were left to their devices save on great occasions. A Government which touches every individual and interferes with him to some extent in daily life, though much esteemed by Europeans, seems intolerable to the Oriental. I had a vision of the tortured peoples of the earth impelled by their own misery to desolate the happy peoples, a vision which grew clearer in the after years. But in that easy-going Eastern life there is a power of resistance, as everybody knows who tries to change it, which may yet defeat the hosts of joyless drudgery.

My Syrian friend—the Suleymân of the following sketches—introduced me to the only Europeans who espoused that life—a French Alsatian family, the Baldenspergers, renowned as pioneers of scientific bee-keeping in Palestine, who hospitably took a share in my initiation. They had innumerable hives in different parts of the country—I have seen them near the Jaffa gardens and among the mountains south of Hebron—which they transported in due season, on the backs of camels, seeking a new growth of flowers. For a long while the Government ignored their industry, until the rumour grew that it was very profitable. Then a high tax was imposed. The Baldenspergers would not pay it. They said the Government might take the hives if it desired to do so. Soldiers were sent to carry out the seizure. But the bee-keepers had taken out the bottom of each hive, and when the soldiers lifted them, out swarmed the angry bees. The soldiers fled; and after that experience the Government agreed to compromise. I remember well a long day's ride with Emile and Samuel Baldensperger, round by Askelon and Ekron, and the luncheon which a village headman had prepared for us, consisting of a whole sheep, roast and stuffed with nuts and vegetables; and a day with Henri Baldensperger in the Hebron region. The friendships of those days were made for life. Hanauer, the Baldenspergers, Suleymân, and other natives of the country—those of them who are alive—remain my friends today.

In short, I ran completely wild for months, in a manner unbecoming to an Englishman; and when at length, upon a pressing invitation, I turned up in Jerusalem and used my introductions, it was in semi-native garb and with a love for Arabs which, I was made to understand, was hardly decent. My native friends were objects of suspicion. I was told that they were undesirable, and, when I stood up for them, was soon put down by the retort that I was very young. I could not obviously claim as much experience as my mature advisers, whose frequent warnings to me to distrust the people of the country thus acquired the force of moral precepts, which it is the secret joy of youth to disobey.

That is the reason why the respectable English residents in Syria figure in these pages as censorious and hostile, with but few exceptions. They were hostile to my point of view, which was not then avowed, but not to me. Indeed, so many of them showed me kindness—particularly in my times of illness—that I cannot think of them without a glow of friendliness. But the attitude of most of them was never mine, and the fact that at the time I still admired that attitude as the correct one, and thought myself at intervals a sad backslider, made it seem forbidding. In my Oriental life they really were, as here depicted, a disapproving shadow in the background. With one—referred to often in these tales—I was in full agreement. We lived together for some months in a small mountain village, and our friendship then established has remained unbroken. But he, though not alone, was an exception.

Owing to the general verdict on my Arab friends, I led what might be called a double life during the months of my first sojourn in Jerusalem; until Suleymân, the tourist season being ended, came with promise of adventure, when I flung discretion to the winds. We hired two horses and a muleteer, and rode away into the north together. A fortnight later, at the foot of the Ladder of Tyre, Suleymân was forced to leave me, being summoned to his village. I still rode on towards the north, alone with one hired muleteer, a simple soul. A notion of my subsequent adventures may, perhaps, be gathered from the following pages, in which I have embodied fictionally some impressions still remaining clear after the lapse of more than twenty years. A record of small things, no doubt; yet it seems possible that something human may be learnt from such a comic sketch-book of experience which would never be derived from more imposing works.

Rashîd the Fair

The brown plain, swimming in a haze of heat, stretched far away into the distance, where a chain of mountains trenched upon the cloudless sky. Six months of drought had withered all the herbage. Only thistles, blue and yellow, and some thorny bushes had survived; but after the torrential winter rains the whole expanse would blossom like the rose. I traversed the plain afterwards in spring, when cornfields waved for miles around its three mud villages, wild flowers in mad profusion covered its waste places, and scarlet tulips flamed amid its wheat.

Now all was desert. After riding for four days in such a landscape, it was sweet to think upon the journey's end, the city of perennial waters, shady gardens, and the song of birds. I was picturing the scene of our arrival—the shade and the repose, the long, cool drinks, the friendly hum of the bazaars—and wondering what letters I should find awaiting me, all to the tune of 'Onward, Christian soldiers'—for the clip-clap of a horse's hoofs invariably beats out in my brain some tune, the most incongruous, against my will—when a sudden outcry roused me. It came from my companion, a hired muleteer, and sounded angry. The fellow had been riding on ahead. I now saw that he had overtaken other travellers—two men astride of one donkey—and had entered into conversation with them. One of the two, the hindmost, was a Turkish soldier. Except the little group they made together, and a vulture, a mere speck above them in the blue, no other living creature was in sight. Something had happened, for the soldier seemed amused, while my poor man was making gestures of despairing protest. He repeated the loud cry which had disturbed my reverie, then turned his mule and hurried back to meet me.

'My knife!' he bellowed 'My knife!—that grand steel blade which was my honour!—so finely tempered and inlaid!—an heirloom in the family! That miscreant, may Allah cut his life!—I mean the soldier—stole it. He asked to look at it a minute, seeming to admire. I gave it, like the innocent I am. He stuck it in his belt, and asked to see the passport which permitted me to carry weapons. Who ever heard of such a thing in this wild region? He will not give it back, though I entreated. I am your Honour's servant, speak for me and make him give it back! It is an heirloom!' That grey-haired man was crying like a baby.

Now, I was very young, and his implicit trust in my authority enthralled me. I valued his dependence on my manhood more than gold and precious stones. Summoning all the courage I possessed, I clapped spurs to my horse and galloped after the marauder.

'Give back that knife!' I roared. 'O soldier! it is you to whom I speak.'

The soldier turned a studiously guileless face—a handsome face, with fair moustache and a week's beard. He had a roguish eye.

'What knife? I do not understand,' he said indulgently.

'The knife you stole from the muleteer here present.'

'Oh, that!' replied the soldier, with a deprecating laugh: 'That is a thing unworthy of your Honour's notice. The rogue in question is a well-known malefactor. He and I are old acquaintance.'

'By the beard of the Prophet, by the August Koran, I never saw his devil's face until this minute!' bawled the muleteer, who had come up behind me.

'Give back the knife,' I ordered for the second time.

'By Allah, never!' was the cool reply.

'Give it back, I say!'

'No, it cannot be—not even to oblige your Honour, for whose pleasure, Allah knows, I would do almost anything,' murmured the soldier, with a charming smile. 'Demand it not. Be pleased to understand that if it were your Honour's knife I would return it instantly. But that man, as I tell you , is a wretch. It grieves me to behold a person of consideration in such an unbecoming temper upon his account—a dog, no more.'

'If he is a dog, he is my dog for the present; so give back the knife!'

'Alas, beloved, that is quite impossible.'

With a wave of the hand dismissing the whole subject the soldier turned away. He plucked a cigarette out of his girdle and prepared to light it. His companion on the donkey had not turned his head nor shown the slightest interest in the discussion. This had lasted long enough. I knew that in another minute I should have to laugh. If anything remained for me to do it must be done immediately. Whipping my revolver from the holster, I held it close against the rascal's head, yelling: 'Give back the knife this minute, or I kill you !'

The man went limp. The knife came back as quick as lightning. I gave it to the muleteer, who blubbered praise to Allah and made off with it. Equally relieved, I was about to follow when the utterly forlorn appearance of the soldier moved me to open the revolver, showing that it was not loaded. Then my adversary was transfigured. His back straightened, his mouth closed, his eyes regained their old intelligence. He stared at me a moment, half incredulous, and then he laughed. Ah, how that soldier laughed! The owner of the donkey turned and shared his glee. They literally hugged each other, roaring with delight, while the donkey underneath them both jogged dutifully on.

Before a caravanserai in a small valley green with fruit-trees, beside a slender stream whose banks were fringed with oleander, I was sitting waiting for some luncheon when the donkey and its riders came again in sight. The soldier tumbled off on spying me and ran into the inn like one possessed. A minute later he brought out the food which I had ordered and set the table for me in the shade of trees.

'I would not let another serve you ,' he informed me, 'for the love of that vile joke that you put upon me. It was not loaded. After all my fright!... It is a nice revolver. Let me look at it.'

'Aye, look your fill, you shalt not touch it,' was my answer; at which he laughed anew, pronouncing me the merriest of Adam's race.

'But tell me, what would you have done had I refused? It was not loaded. What would you have done?'

His hand was resting at that moment on a stool. I rapped his knuckles gently with the butt of the revolver to let him know its weight.

'*Wallahi!*' he cried out in admiration. 'I believe you would have smashed my head with it. All for the sake of a poor man of no account, who you employ for a week, and after that will see no more. *Efendim*, take me as your servant always!' Of a sudden he spoke very earnestly. 'Pay the money to release me from the army. It is a largish sum—five Turkish pounds. And Allah knows I will repay it to you by my service. For the love of righteousness accept me, for my soul is thine.'

I ridiculed the notion. He persisted. When the muleteer and I set forth again, he rode beside us, mounted on another donkey this time—'borrowed,' as he put it—which showed he was a person of resource. 'By Allah, I can shoe a horse and cook a fowl; I can mend garments with a thread and shoot a bird upon the wing,' he told me. 'I would take care of the stable and the house. I would do everything your Honour wanted. My nickname is Rashîd the Fair; my garrison is Karameyn, just two days' journey from the city. Come in a day or two and buy me out. No matter for the wages. Only try me!'

At the khan, a pretty rough one, where we spent the night, he waited on me deftly and enforced respect, making me really wish for such a servant. On the morrow, after an hour's riding, our ways parted.

'In sh'Allah, I shall see you before many days,' he murmured. 'My nickname is Rashîd the Fair, forget not. I shall tell our captain you are coming with the money.'

I said that I might think about it possibly.

'Come,' he entreated. 'You would never shame a man who puts his trust in you. I say that I shall tell our captain you are coming. Ah, shame me not before the Commandant and all my comrades! You think me a thief, a lawbreaker, because I took that fellow's knife?' he asked, with an indulgent smile. 'Let me tell you , O my lord, that I was in my right and duty as a soldier of the Sultan in this province. It is that muleteer who, truly speaking, breaks the law by carrying the knife without a permit. And you, have you a passport for that fine revolver? At the place where we had luncheon yesterday were other soldiers. By merely calling on them to support me I could have had his knife and your revolver with ease and honesty in strict accordance with the law. Why did I not do so? Because I love you! Say you will come to Karameyn and buy me out.'

I watched him jogging on his donkey towards a gulley of the hills along which lay the bridle-path to Karameyn. On all the evidence he was a rogue, and yet my intimate conviction was that he was honest. All the Europeans in the land would lift up hands of horror and exclaim: 'Beware!' on hearing such a story. Yet, as I rode across the parched brown land towards the city of green trees and rushing waters, I knew that I should go to Karameyn.

A Mountain Garrison

The long day's ride was uneventful, but not so the night. I spent it in a village of the mountains at a very curious hostelry, kept by a fat native Christian, named Elias, who laid claim, upon the signboard, to furnish food and lodging *'alafranga'*—that is, in the modern European manner. There was one large guest-room, and an adjoining bedroom of the same dimensions, for some thirty travellers. I had to find a stable for my horse elsewhere. A dining-table was provided, and we sat on chairs around it; but the food was no wise European, and the cooking was degraded Greek. A knife, fork, and spoon were laid for every guest but several cast these on the floor and used their fingers. In the long bedroom were a dozen beds on bedsteads. By offering a trifle extra I secured one to myself. In others there were two, three, even four together. An elderly Armenian gentleman who had a wife with him, stood guard with pistols over her all night. He was so foolish as to threaten loudly anyone who dared approach her. After he had done so several times a man arose from the bed next to mine and strolling to him seized him by the throat.

'O man,' he chided. 'Are you mad or what, thus to arouse our passions by your talk of women? Be silent, or we honest men here present will wring your neck and take your woman from you . Do you understand?' He shook that jealous husband as a terrier would shake a rat. 'Be silent, hear you? Men wish to sleep.'

'Said I not well, O brother?' said the monitor to me, as he got back to bed.

'By Allah, well,' was my reply. The jealous one was silent after that. But there were other noises. Some men still lingered in the guest-room playing cards. The host, devoted to things European, had a musical-box—it was happily before the day of gramophones—which the card-players kept going all night long. I had a touch of fever. There were insects. Sleep was hopeless. I rose while it was yet night, went out without paying, since the host was nowhere to be seen, and, in some danger from the fierce attacks of pariah dogs, found out the vault in which my horse was stabled. Ten minutes later I was clear of the village, riding along a mountain side but dimly visible beneath the stars. The path descended to a deep ravine, and rose again, up, up, interminably. At length, upon the summit of a ridge, I felt the dawn. The mountain tops were whitened like the crests of waves, while all the clefts and hollows remained full of night. Behind me, in the east, there was a long white streak making the mountain outlines bleak and keen. The stars looked strange; a fresh breeze fanned my cheek and rustled in the grass and shrubs. Before me, on an isolated bluff, appeared my destination, a large village, square-built like a fortress. Its buildings presently took on a wild-rose blush, which deepened to the red of fire—a splendid sight against a dark blue sky, still full of stars. A window flashed up there. The sun had risen.

Some English people, when informed of my intention to buy a man out of the Turkish Army had pronounced it madness. I did not know the people of the land as they did. I should be pillaged, brought to destitution, perhaps murdered. They, who had lived in the country twenty, thirty years, were better qualified to judge than I was. For peace and quiet I pretended acquiescence, and my purpose thus acquired a taste of stealth. It was with the feelings of a kind of truant that I had set out at length without a word to anyone, and with the same adventurous feelings that I now drew near to Karameyn. Two soldiers, basking in the sunshine on a dust-heap, sprang up at my approach. One was the man I sought, the rogue Rashîd. They led me to their captain's house—a modest dwelling, consisting of a single room, with hardly any furniture. A score of soldiers followed after us.

The Captain—Hasan Agha—an old man, with face scarred and heavy white moustache, was in full uniform, and, as I entered, was engaged in putting on a pair of cotton gloves. He was one of the old *'alaïli,'* Turkish officers—those whose whole knowledge of their business was derived from service in a regiment or *'alaï,'* instead of from instruction at a military school; and his manner towards the men had nothing of the martinet. He addressed them as 'my children,' with affection; and they, though quite respectful, conversed freely in his presence. Hasan Agha paid me many compliments, and repeatedly inquired after my health. He would not hear about my business till I had had breakfast. Luncheon had been arranged for me, he said, but that could not be ready for some hours. Would I be so kind as to excuse a makeshift? Even as he spoke, a soldier entered with a tray on which were slabs of Arab bread, a pitcher of sour milk, and heaps of grapes. Another soldier began pounding coffee, while yet another blew upon the charcoal in a brazier. I refused to eat unless my host ate with me, which he did only after much polite resistance. After the meal, we sat and talked, the soldiers joining in the conversation. They told me of old wars and deeds of valour. Hasan Agha was, it seemed, a famous fighter; and the men did all they could to make him tell me of his battles. They brought an old man in out of the town to see me because he had fought in the Crimean war, and knew the English. Before it grew too hot, they

took me out to see the barracks and a ramshackle old
fieldpiece which they seemed to idolise. Then followed
luncheon with its long array of Arab dishes, of which the
soldiers had their share eventually. Rashîd assured me
afterwards that all the food on this occasion had been
'borrowed.' That was in Abdul Hamid's golden days. After
luncheon, there was coffee with more compliments; and
then at last we got to business.

A public writer was brought in. He wrote out a receipt
for me, and also the discharge Rashîd required. Hasan
Agha stamped both documents with an official seal, and
handed them to me, who gave him in exchange the
money.

'Bismillah!' he exclaimed. 'I call all here to witness that
Rashîd, the son of Ali, called the Fair, is free henceforth to
go what way he chooses.'

To me he said: 'Rashîd is a good lad, and you will find
him useful. The chief fault I have found in him is this: that,
when obeying orders, he is apt to think, and so invent a
method of his own, not always good. Also, he is too
susceptible to female charms, a failing which has placed
him in some strange positions.'

The last remark evoked much laughter, relating, evidently
to some standing joke unknown to me. Rashîd looked
rather sheepish. Hasan Agha turned to him, and said:

'My son, praise Allah for your great good fortune in
finding favour in the sight of one so noble and benevolent
as our beloved guest, who is henceforth your master.
Remember, he is not as I am—one who has been what you
are, and so knows the tricks. Serve him freely with your
mind and soul and conscience, not waiting for commands
as in the Army. Come hither, O my son, grasp hands with
me. I say, may God be with you now and always! Forget not

all the good instruction of your soldier days. Be sure that we shall pray for your good master and for you .'

The old man's eyes were wet, so were Rashîd's, so were the eyes of all the soldiers squatting round.

Rashîd, dismissed, went off to change his uniform for an old suit of mine which I had brought for him, while Hasan Agha, talking of him as a father might, explained to me his character and little failings.

At last I took my leave. Rashîd was waiting in my cast-off clothes, a new fez of civilian shape upon his head. He held my stirrup, and then jumped on to a raw-boned beast which had been 'borrowed' for him by his friends, so he informed me. It might be worth my while to buy it for him, he suggested later—the price was only eight pounds Turk, the merest trifle. The whole garrison escorted us to the last houses, where they stood a long while, waving their farewells. Two hours later, on the mountain-ridge, beyond the *wady*, we turned to look our last on Karameyn. It stood amid the flames of sunset like a castle of the clouds.

We returned, then, to the *'alafranga'* hostelry; but Rashîd, having heard the story of my sleepless night, would not allow me to put up there. I paid my debt to the proprietor, and then he found for me an empty house to which he brought a mattress and a coverlet, a lot of cushions, a brazier, and the things required for making coffee, also a tray of supper—all of them borrowed from the neighbouring houses. I might be pillaged, brought to destitution, and eventually murdered by him, as my friends had warned me. At least, the operation promised to be comfortable.

THE RHINOCEROS WHIP

'Where is the whip?' Rashîd cried, suddenly, turning upon me in the gateway of the *khan* where we had just arrived.

'Merciful Allah! It is not with me. I must have left it in the carriage.'

Rashîd threw down the saddlebags, our customary luggage, which he had been carrying, and started running for his life. The carriage had got half-way down the narrow street half-roofed with awnings. At Rashîd's fierce shout of 'Wait, O my uncle! We have left our whip!' the driver turned and glanced behind him, but, instead of stopping, lashed his horses to a gallop. Rashîd ran even faster than before. The chase, receding rapidly, soon vanished from my sight. Twilight was coming on. Above the low, flat roofs to westward, the crescent moon hung in the green of sunset behind the minarets of the great mosque. I then took up the saddle-bags and delicately picked my way through couchant camels, tethered mules and horses in the courtyard to the *khan* itself, which was a kind of cloister. I was making my arrangements with the landlord, when Rashîd returned, the picture of despair. He flung up both his hands, announcing failure, and then sank down upon the ground and moaned. The host, a burly man, inquired what ailed him. I told him, when he uttered just reflections upon cabmen and the vanity of worldly wealth. Rashîd, as I could see, was '*zi'lân*'—a prey to that strange mixture of mad rage and sorrow and despair, which is a real disease for children of the Arabs. An English servant would not thus have cared about the loss of a small item of his master's property, not by his fault but through that master's oversight. But my possessions were Rashîd's delight, his claim to honour. He boasted of them to all comers. In particular did he revere my gun, my Service revolver, and this whip—a tough thong of rhinoceros hide, rather nicely mounted with silver, which had been presented to me by an aged Arab in return for some imagined favour. I had found it useful against pariah dogs when these rushed out in packs to bite one's horse's legs, but had never viewed it as a badge of honour till Rashîd came to me. To him it was the best of our possessions, marking us as of rank above the common. He thrust it on me even when I went out walking; and he it was who, when we started from our mountain home at noon that day, had laid it reverently down upon the seat beside me before he climbed upon the box beside the driver. And now the whip was lost through my neglectfulness. Rashîd's dejection made me feel a worm.

'Allah! Allah!' he made moan, 'What can I do? The driver was a chance encounter. I do not know his dwelling, which may God destroy!'

The host remarked in comfortable tones that flesh is grass, all treasure perishable, and that it behoves a man to fix desire on higher things. Whereat Rashîd sprang up, as one past patience, and departed, darting through the cattle in the yard with almost supernatural agility. 'Let him eat his rage alone!' the host advised me, with a shrug.

Having ordered supper for the third hour of the night, I, too, went out to stretch my limbs, which were stiff and bruised from four hours' jolting in a springless carriage, always on the point of overturning. We should have done better to have come on horseback in the usual way; but

Rashîd, having chanced upon the carriage, a great rarity, had decided on that way of going as more fashionable, forgetful of the fact that there was not a road.

The stars were out. In the few shops which still kept open lanterns hung, throwing streaks of yellow light on the uneven causeway, a gleam into the eyes of wayfarers and prowling dogs. Many of the people in the streets, too, carried lanterns whose swing made objects in their circle seem to leap and fall. I came at length into an open place where there was concourse—a kind of square which might be called the centre of the city.

The crowd there, as I noticed with surprise, was stationary, with all its faces turned in one direction. I heard a man's voice weeping and declaiming wildly.

'What is it?' I inquired, among the outskirts.

'A great misfortune!' someone answered. 'A poor servant has lost a whip worth fifty Turkish pounds, his master's property. It was stolen from him by a miscreant—a wicked cabman. His lord will kill him if he fails to find it.'

Seized with interest, I shouldered my way forward. There was Rashîd against the wall of a large mosque, beating himself against that wall with a most fearful outcry. A group of high-fezzed soldiers, the policemen of the city, hung round him in compassion, questioning. Happily, I wore a fez, and so was inconspicuous.

'Fifty Turkish pounds!' he yelled. 'A hundred would not buy its brother! My master, the tremendous Count of all the English—their chief prince, by Allah!—loves it as his soul. He will pluck out and devour my heart and liver. O High Protector! O Almighty Lord!'

'What like was this said cabman?' asked a sergeant of the watch.

Rashîd, with sobs and many pious interjections, described the cabman rather neatly as 'a one-eyed man, full-bearded, of a form as if inflated in the lower half. His name, he told me, was Habîb; but Allah knows!'

'The man is known!' exclaimed the sergeant, eagerly. 'His dwelling is close by. Come, O you poor, ill-used one. We will take the whip from him.'

At that Rashîd's grief ceased as if by magic. He took the sergeant's hand and fondled it, as they went off together. I followed with the crowd as far as to the cabman's door, a filthy entry in a narrow lane, where, wishing to avoid discovery, I broke away and walked back quickly to the *khan*.

I had been there in my private alcove some few minutes, when Rashîd arrived with a triumphant air, holding on high the famous whip. The sergeant came across the court with him. A score of soldiers waited in the gateway as I could see by the light of the great lantern hanging from the arch.

'Praise be to Allah, I have found it!' cried Rashîd.

'Praise be to Allah, we have been enabled to do a little service for your Highness,' cried the sergeant. Therewith he pounced upon my hand and kissed it. I made them both sit down and called for coffee. Between the two of them, I heard the story. The sergeant praised Rashîd's intelligence in going out and crying in a public place until the city and its whole police force had a share in his distress. Rashîd, on his side, said that all that would have been in vain but for the sergeant's knowledge of the cabman's house. The sergeant, with a chuckle, owned that that same knowledge would have been of no effect had not Rashîd once more displayed his keen intelligence. They had poured into the house—a single room, illumined only by a saucer lamp upon the ground—and searched it thoroughly, the cabman all the while protesting his great innocence, and swearing he had never in this world beheld a whip like that described. The soldiers, finding no whip, were beginning to believe his word when Rashîd, who had remained aloof, observing that the cabman's wife stood very still beneath her veils, assailed her with a mighty push, which sent her staggering across the room. The whip was then discovered. It had been hidden underneath her petticoats. They had given the delinquent a good beating then and there. Would that be punishment enough in my opinion? asked the sergeant.

We decided that the beating was enough. I gave the sergeant a small present when he left. Rashîd went with him, after carefully concealing the now famous whip. I suppose they went off to some tavern to discuss the wonderful adventure more at length; for I supped alone, and had been some time stretched upon my mattress on the floor before Rashîd came in and spread his bed beside me.

'Art you awake, O my dear lord?' he whispered. 'By Allah, you did wrong to give that sergeant any money. I had made your name so great that but to look on you was fee sufficient for a poor, lean dog like him.'

He then was silent for so long a while that I imagined he had gone to sleep. But, suddenly, he whispered once again:

'O my dear lord, forgive me the disturbance, but have you our revolver safe?'

'By Allah, yes! Here, ready to my hand.'

'Good. But it would be better for the future that I should bear our whip and our revolver. I have made your name so great that you should carry nothing.'

The Courteous Judge

We were giving a dinner-party on that day to half a dozen Turkish officers, and, when he brought me in my cup of tea at seven-thirty a.m., Rashîd informed me that our cook had been arrested. The said cook was a decent Muslim, but hot-tempered, and something of a blood in private life. At six a.m., as he stood basking in the sunlight in our doorway, his eyes had fallen on some Christian youths upon their way to college, in European clothes, with new kid gloves and silver-headed canes. Maddened with a sense of outrage by that horrid sight, he had attacked the said youths furiously with a wooden ladle, putting them to flight, and chasing them all down the long acacia avenue, through two suburbs into the heart of the city, where their miserable cries for help brought the police upon him. Rashîd, pursuing in vain attempts to calm the holy warrior, had seen him taken into custody still flourishing the ladle; but could tell me nothing of his after fate, having at that point deemed it prudent to retire, lest he, too, might be put in prison by mistake.

It was sad. As soon as I was up and dressed, I wrote to Hamdi Bey, the chief of our intended visitors, informing him of the mishap which would prevent our giving him and his comrades a dinner at all worthy of their merit. By the time that I had finished dressing, Rashîd had found a messenger to whom the note was given with an order to make haste. He must have run the whole way there and back, for, after little more than half an hour, he stood before me, breathless and with streaming brow, his bare legs dusty to the knee. Rashîd had then gone out to do some marketing. The runner handed me a note. It said:

'Why mention such a trifling detail? We shall, of course, be charmed with anything you set before us. It is for friendship, not for food, we come!'

There was a postscript:—

'Why not go and see the judge?'

Suleymân was in the room. He was an old acquaintance, a man of decent birth, but poor, by trade a dragoman, who had acquired a reputation for unusual wisdom. When he had nothing else to do, he came to me unfailingly, wherever I might chance to be established or encamped. He was sitting cross-legged in a corner, smoking his narghîleh, capriciously illumined by thin slants of light, alive with motes, from the Venetian blinds. He seized upon the postscript, crying:—

'It is good advice. Why not, indeed? Let us approach the judge.'

Therewith he coiled the tube of his *narghîleh* carefully around the bowl thereof, and, rising with the same deliberation, threw upon his shoulders a white dust-cloak, then looked at me, and questioned: 'Are you ready?'

'But I do not know the judge.'

'No more do I. But that, my dear, is a disease which can be remedied.'

Without much trouble we found out the judge's house. A servant told us that his Honour had already started for the court. We took a carriage and pursued his Honour. At the court we made inquiry of the crowd of witnesses—false witnesses for hire—who thronged the entrance. The judge, we heard, had not yet taken his seat. We should be sure to

find his Honour in the coffee-shop across the road. One
of the false witnesses conducted us to the said coffee-shop
and pointed out our man. Together with his clerk and
certain advocates, one of whom read aloud the morning
news, the judge sat underneath a vine arbour in pleasant
shade. He smiled. His hands were clasped upon a fair
round belly.

Suleymân, his dust-cloak billowing, strolled forward
coolly, and presented me as 'one of the chief people of the
Franks.' The company arose and made us welcome, placing
stools for our convenience.

'His Highness comes to you for justice, O most righteous
judge. He has been wronged,' observed Suleymân,
dispassionately.

The judge looked much concerned. 'What is the case?' he
asked.

'Our cook is snatched from us,' was the reply, 'and
tonight we have invited friends to dinner.'

'Is he a good cook?' asked the judge, with feeling.

'If your Excellency will restore him to us, and then join
us at the meal——'

'How can I be of service in this matter?'

I motioned to Suleymân to tell the story, which he did so
well that all the company were soon in fits of laughter.

The judge looked through the cause list till he found the
case, putting a mark against it on the paper.

'How can we dine tonight without a cook?' I sighed,
despairingly.

'Fear nothing,' said the judge. 'He shall be with you in an
hour. Come, O my friends, we must to business! It grows
late.'

The judge took leave of me with much politeness.

'Now,' said Suleymân, when they were gone, 'let us go into the court and watch the course of justice.'

We crossed the narrow street to an imposing portal. Suleymân whispered to a soldier there on guard, who smiled and bade us enter, with a gracious gesture.

The hall inside was crowded. Only after much exertion could we see the dais. There sat the judge, and there stood our lamented cook, the picture of dejection. A soldier at his side displayed the wooden ladle. The Christian dandies whom he had assaulted were giving their account of the adventure volubly, until his Honour, with a heavy frown, bade them be silent. Then they cowered.

'Be careful what you say,' the judge enjoined. 'You have not hesitated to impute the anger of this cook to religious fanaticism. The Nazarenes are much too ready to bring such a charge against the Muslims, forgetful that there may be other causes of annoyance. Nay, many of the charges brought have proved upon investigation to be altogether groundless. You Nazarenes are often insolent in your demeanour. Confiding in the favour of the foreign consuls, foreign missionaries, you occasionally taunt and irritate, even revile, the Muslims. Now, even supposing your account of this affair to be correct—which I much doubt, for, on the one hand, I behold a wooden ladle of no weight; while, on the other, there are two fine walking-sticks with silver heads'—one of the Christian youths let fall his stick in trepidation—'and you are two, while this poor cook is one. Even supposing what you say is true, are you certain that nothing in your appearance, conversation, or behaviour gave him cause for anger? I incline to conjecture that you must have flouted him, or uttered, it may be, some insult to his creed.'

'He beat us for no reason, and most grievously,' moaned one of the assailed. Such language from a Muslim judge in a court filled with Muslims made the two Christians tremble in their shoes.

'We did not even see him till he started beating us. By Allah, my poor head is sore, my back is broken with that awful beating. He was like a madman!' The speaker and his fellow-plaintiff wept aloud.

'Did you beat these youths, as he describes?' inquired the judge, turning towards the cook with like severity.

'No, O Excellency!' came the bitter cry. 'I am an ill-used man, much slandered. I never set eyes upon those men until this minute.' He also began weeping bitterly.

'Both parties tell me lies!' exclaimed the judge, with anger. 'For you, O cook, did beat these youths. The fact is known, for you were taken in the act of beating them. And you, O Nazarenes, are not much injured, for everyone beholds you in most perfect health, with clothes unspoilt. The more shame to you, for it is evident that you bring the charge against this Muslim from religious hatred.'

'By Allah, no, O Excellency. We wish that man no harm. We did but state what happened.'

'You are a pack of rogues together,' roared the judge. 'Let each side pay one whole *mejîdi* to the court; let the parties now, this minute, here before me, swear peace and lifelong friendship for the future, and never let me hear of them again!'

The Christian youths embraced the cook, the cook embraced the Christian youths repeatedly, all weeping in a transport of delight at their escape from punishment. I paid the money for our man, who then went home with us; Suleymân, upon the way, delivering a lecture of such high morality, such heavenly language, that the poor, simple fellow wept anew, and called on Allah for forgiveness.

'Repentance is your duty,' said Suleymân approvingly. 'But towards this world also you can make amends. Put forth your utmost skill in cookery this evening, for the judge is coming.'

NAWÂDIR †

We had arrived in a village of the mountains late one afternoon, and were sauntering about the place, when some rude children shouted: 'Hi, O my uncle, you have come in two!'

It was the common joke at sight of European trousers, which were rare in those days. But Suleymân was much offended upon my account. He turned about and read those children a tremendous lecture, rebuking them severely for thus presuming to insult a stranger and a guest. His condemnation was supported on such lofty principles as no man who possessed a particle of religion or good feeling could withstand; and his eloquence was so commanding yet persuasive that, when at length he moved away, not children only but many also of the grown-up people followed him.

The village was high up beneath the summit of a ridge, and from a group of rocks within a stone's throw of it could be seen the sea, a great blue wall extending north and south. We perched among those rocks to watch the sunset. The village people settled within earshot, some below and some above us. Presently an old man said:

'You speak well, O sage! It is a sin for them to cry such things behind a guest of quality. Their misbehaviour calls for strong correction. But I truly think that no child who has heard your Honour's sayings will ever be so impudent again.'

† *Rare things*

'Amân!' (peace) cried one of the delinquents. 'Allah knows that our intention was not very evil.'

I hastened to declare that the offence was nothing. But Suleymân would not allow me to decry it.

'Your Honour is as yet too young,' he said severely, 'to understand the mystic value of men's acts and words. A word may be well meant and innocent, and yet the cause of much disaster, possessing in itself some special virtue of malignity. You all know how the *jânn* attend on careless words; how if I call a goat, a dog, or cat by its generic name without pointing to the very animal intended, a *jinni* will as like as not attach himself to me, since many of the *jânn* are called by names of animals. You all know also that to praise the beauty of a child, without the offer of that child to Allah as a sacrifice, is fatal; because there is unseen a jealous listener who hates and would deform the progeny of Eve. Such facts as those are known to every ignoramus, and their cause is plain. But there exists another and more subtle danger in the careless use of words, particularly with regard to personal remarks, like that of these same children when they cried to our good master: 'You have come in two,' directing the attention to a living body. I have a rare thing in my memory which perhaps may lead you to perceive my meaning darkly.

'A certain husbandman *(fellâh)* was troubled with a foolish wife. Having to go out one day, he gave her full instructions what to do about the place, and particularly bade her fix her mind upon their cow, because he was afraid the cow might stray, as she had done before, and cause ill-feeling with the neighbours. He never thought that such a charge to such a person, tending to concentrate the woman's mind upon a certain object, was disastrous. The man meant well; the woman, too, meant well. She gave her whole mind to obey his parting words. Having completed every task within the house, she sat down under an olive tree which grew before the door, and fixed her whole intelligence in all its force upon the black-and-white cow, the only living thing in sight, which was browsing in the space allowed by a short tether. So great did the responsibility appear to her that she grew anxious, and by dint of earnest gazing at the cow came to believe that there was something wrong with it. In truth the poor beast had exhausted all the grass within its reach, and it had not entered her ideas to move the picket.

'At length a neighbour passed that way. She begged him, of his well-known kindness, to inspect the cow and tell her what the matter really was. This neighbour was a wag, and knew the woman's species; he also knew the cow as an annoyance, forever dragging out its peg and straying into planted fields. After long and serious examination he declared: "The tail is hurting her and ought to be removed. See how she swishes it from side to side. If the tail is not cut off immediately, the cow will die one day."

"'Merciful Allah!" cried the woman. "Please remove it for me. I am all alone, and helpless."

'The man lifted up an axe which he was carrying and cut off the cow's tail near the rump. He gave it to the woman and she thanked him heartily. He went his way, while she resumed her watch upon the cow. And still she fancied that its health was not as usual.

'Another neighbour came along. She told him of her fears, and how the Sheykh Mukarram, of his well-known kindness, had befriended her by cutting off the damaged tail.

"Of course," cried the newcomer, "that accounts for it! The animal is now ill-balanced. It is always a mistake to take from one end without removing something also from the other. If you would see that cow in health again, the horns must go."

"Oh, help me; I am all alone! Perform the operation for me," said the woman.

'Her friend sawed off the horns and gave them to her. She exhausted thanks. But still, when he was gone, the cow appeared no better. She grew desperate.

'By then the news of her anxiety about the cow had spread through all the village, and every able body came to help her or look on. They cut the udder and the ears, and then the legs, and gave them to her, and she thanked them all with tears of gratitude. At last there was no cow at all to worry over. Seeing the diminished carcase lying motionless, the woman smiled and murmured: "Praise to Allah, she is cured at last; she is at rest! Now I am free to go into the house and get things ready for my lord's return."

'Her lord returned at dusk. She told him: "I have been obedient. I watched the cow and tended her for hours. She was extremely ill, but all the neighbours helped to doctor her, performing many operations, and we were able to relieve her of all pain, the praise to Allah! Here are the various parts which they removed. They gave them to me, very kindly, since the cow is ours."

'Without a word the man went out to view the remnant of the cow. When he returned he seized the woman by the shoulders, and, gazing straight into her eyes, said grimly: "Allah keep you ! I am going to walk this world until I find one filthier than you. And if I fail to find one filthier than you, I shall go on walking—I have sworn it—to the end."'

Suleymân broke off there suddenly, to the surprise of all.

'I fail to see how that rare thing applies to my case,' I

observed, as soon as I felt sure that he had finished speaking.

'It does not apply to your case, but it does to others,' he replied on brief reflection. 'It is dangerous to put ideas in people's heads or rouse self-consciousness, for who can tell what demons lurk in people's brains.... But wait and I will find a rare thing suited to the present instance.'

'Say, O Sea of Wisdom, did he find one filthier than she was?'

'Of course he did.'

'Relate the sequel, I beseech you.'

But Suleymân was searching in his memory for some event more clearly illustrating the grave risks of chance suggestion. At length he gave a sigh of satisfaction, and then spoke as follows:

'There was once a Turkish pasha of the greatest renown, a benevolent old man, whom I have often seen. He had a long white beard, of which he was extremely proud, until one day a man, who was a wag, came up to him and said:

'"Excellency, we have been wondering: When you go to bed, do you put your beard inside the coverings or out?"

'The Pasha thought a moment, but he could not tell, for it had never come into his head to notice such a matter. He promised to inform his questioner upon the morrow. But when he went to bed that night he tried the beard beneath the bedclothes and above without success. Neither could he get comfort, nor could he, for the life of him, remember how the beard was wont to go. He got no sleep on that night or the next night either, for thinking on the problem thus presented to his mind. On the third day, in a rage, he called a barber and had the beard cut off. Accustomed as he was to such a mass of hair upon his neck, for lack of it he caught a cold and died.

'That story fits the case before us to a nicety,' said Suleymân in conclusion, with an air of triumph.

'What is the moral of it, deign to tell us, master!' the cry arose from all sides in the growing twilight.

'I suppose,' I hazarded, 'that, having had attention called to the peculiar clothing of my legs, I shall eventually have them amputated or wear Turkish trousers?'

'I say not what will happen; God alone knows that. But the mere chance that such catastrophes, as I have shown, may happen is enough to make wise people shun that kind of speech.'

I cannot to this day distinguish how much of his long harangue was jest and how much earnest. But the *fellâhîn* devoured it as pure wisdom.

'What happened to the man who went to seek one filthier than she was? How could he ever find one filthier?' inquired Rashîd, reverting to Suleymân's unfinished story of the foolish woman and her husband and the hapless cow, when we lay down to sleep that evening in the village guest-room. I also asked to hear the rest of that instructive tale. Suleymân, sufficiently besought, raised himself upon an elbow and resumed the narrative. Rashîd and I lay quiet in our wrappings.

'We had reached that point, my masters, where the injured husband, having seen the remnant of the cow, said to his wife: "Now, I am going to walk this world until I find one filthier than you are; and if I fail to find one filthier than you are I shall go on walking till I die." Well, he walked and he walked—for months, some people say, and others years—until he reached a village in Mount Lebanon—a village of the Maronites renowned for foolishness. It was the reputation of their imbecility which made him go there.'

'What was his name?' inquired Rashîd, who liked to have things clear.

'His name?' said Suleymân reflectively, 'was Sâlih.'

'He was a Muslim?'

'Aye, a Muslim, I suppose—though, Allah knows, he may perhaps have been an Ismaîli or a Druze. Any more questions? Then I will proceed.

'He came into this village of the Maronites, and, being thirsty, looked in at a doorway. He saw the village priest and all his family engaged in stuffing a fat sheep with mulberry leaves. The sheep was tethered half-way up the steps which led on to the housetop. The priest and his wife, together with their eldest girl, sat on the ground below, amid a heap of mulberry boughs; and all the other children sat, one on every step, passing up the leaves, when ready, to the second daughter, whose business was to force the sheep to go on eating. This they would do until the sheep, too full to stand, fell over on its side, when they would slaughter it for their supply of fat throughout the coming year.

'So busy were they in this occupation that they did not see the stranger in the doorway until he shouted: "Peace upon this house," and asked them for a drink of water kindly. Even then the priest did not disturb himself, but, saying "*Itfaddal!*" pointed to a pitcher standing by the wall. The guest looked into it and found it dry.

'"No water here," he said.

'"Oh," sighed the priest, "today we are so thirsty with this work that we have emptied it, and so busy that the children have forgotten to refill it. Rise, O Nesîbeh, take the pitcher on your head, and hasten to the spring and bring back water for our guest."

'The girl Nesîbeh, who was fourteen years of age, rose

up obediently, shaking off the mulberry leaves and caterpillars from her clothing. Taking up the pitcher, she went out through the village to the spring, which gushed out of the rock beneath a spreading pear tree.

'There were so many people getting water at the moment that she could not push her way among them, so sat down to wait her turn, choosing a shady spot. She was a thoughtful girl, and, as she sat there waiting, she was saying in her soul:

'"O soul, I am a big girl now. A year or two and mother will unite me to a proper husband. The next year I shall have a little son. Again a year or two, he will be big enough to run about; and his father will make for him a pair of small red shoes, and he will come down to this pleasant spring, as children do, to splash the water. Being a bold lad, he will climb that tree."

'And then, as she beheld one great bough overhanging like a stretched-out arm, and realised how dangerous it was for climbing children, she thought:

'"He will fall down and break his neck."

'At once she burst out weeping inconsolably, making so great a din that all the people who had come for water flocked around her, asking: "O Nesîbeh, what has hurt you?" And between her sobs, she told them:

'"I'm a big girl, now."

'"That is so, O beloved!"

'"A year or two, and mother will provide me with a husband."

'"It is likely."

'"Another year, and I shall have a little son."

'"If God wills!" sighed the multitude, with pious fervour.

"'Again a year or two, he will be big enough to run about, and his father will make for him a pair of small red shoes. And he will come down to the spring with other children, and will climb the tree. And—oh!—you see that big bough overhanging. There he will slip and fall and break his neck! Ah, woe!"

'At that the people cried: "O cruel fate!" and many of them rent their clothes. They all sank down upon the ground around Nesîbeh, rocking themselves to and fro and wailing:

"'Ah, my little neighbour. My poor, dear little neighbour! Ah, would that you had lived to bury me, my little neighbour!" †

'Meanwhile the stranger waiting for the water grew impatient, and he once more ventured to interrupt the work of sheep-stuffing with a remark that the young girl was long returning with her pitcher. The priest said: "That is true," and sent his second daughter to expedite the first. This girl went running to the spring, and found the population of the village sitting weeping on the ground around her sister. She asked the matter. They replied: "A great calamity! Thy sister—poor distracted mother!—will inform you of its nature." She ran up to Nesîbeh, who moaned out: "I am a big girl now. A year or two, our mother will provide me with a husband. The next year I shall have a little son. Again a year or two he will be old enough to run about. His father will make for him a pair of small red shoes. He comes down to the spring to play in childish wise. He climbs that tree, and from that over-hanging branch he falls and breaks his neck."

'At this sad news the second girl forgot her errand. She threw her skirt over her head and started shrieking: "Alas, my

† *Yâ takbar jârak, yâ jârï!*—a very common cry of grief in Syria.

little nephew! My poor, dear little nephew! Would God that you had lived to bury me, my little nephew!" And she too sat down upon the ground to hug her sorrow with the rest.

'The priest said: "That one too is long in coming; I will send another child; but you must take her place upon the steps, O stranger, or else the work of stuffing will be much delayed."

'The stranger did as he was asked, while child after child was sent, till he alone was left to do the work of carrying the fresh leaves up from the ground and stuffing them into the sheep. Still none returned.

'The priest's wife went herself, remarking that her husband and the stranger were able by themselves to carry on the work. They did so a long while, yet no one came.

'At last the priest rose, saying: "I myself will go and beat them for this long delay. Do thou, O stranger, feed the sheep meanwhile. Cease not to carry up the leaves and stuff him with them, lest all the good work done be lost through negligence."

'In anger the priest strode out through the village to the spring. But all his wrath was changed into amazement when he saw the crowd of people sitting on the ground, convulsed with grief, around the members of his family.

'He went up to his wife and asked the matter.

'She moaned: "I cannot speak of it. Ask poor Nesîbeh!"

'He then turned to his eldest daughter, who, half-choked by sobs, explained:

"'I am a big girl now."

"'That is so, O my daughter."

"'A year or two, and you and mother will provide me with a husband."

'"That is possible."

'"Another year, and I shall have a little son!"

'"*In sh'Allah!*" said her father piously.

'"Again a year or two, and my son runs about. His father makes for him a pair of small red shoes. He came down to the spring to play with other children, and from that overhanging bough—how shall I tell it?—he fell and broke his darling little neck!" Nesîbeh hid her face again and wailed aloud.

'The priest, cut to the heart by the appalling news, tore his cassock up from foot to waist, and threw the ends over his face, vociferating:

'"Woe, my little grandson! My darling little grandson! Oh, would that you had lived to bury me, my little grandson!" And he too sank upon the ground, immersed in grief.

'At last the stranger wearied of the work of stripping off the mulberry leaves and carrying them up the staircase to the tethered sheep. He found his thirst increased by such exertions.'

'Did he in truth do that, with no one looking?' said Rashîd. 'He must have been as big a fool as all the others.'

'He was, but in a different way,' said Suleymân.

'He walked down to the spring, and saw the congregation seated underneath the pear tree, shrieking like sinners at the Judgment Day. Among them sat the priest, with features hidden in his torn black petticoat. He ventured to approach the man and put a question. The priest unveiled his face a moment and was going to speak, but recollection of his sorrow overcame him. Hiding his face again, he wailed:

'"Alas, my little grandson! My pretty little grandson! Ah, would that you had lived to bury me, my little grandson!"

'A woman sitting near plucked at the stranger's sleeve and said:

'"You see that girl. She will be soon full-grown. A year or two, and she will certainly be married. Another year, and she will have a little son. Her little son grows big enough to run about. His father made for him a pair of small red shoes. He came down to the spring to play with other children. You see that pear tree? On a day like this—a pleasant afternoon—he clambered up it, and from that bough, which overhangs the fountain, he fell and broke his little neck upon those stones. Alas, our little neighbour! Oh, would that you had lived to bury us, our little neighbour!" And everyone began to rock and wail anew.

'The stranger stood and looked upon them for a moment, then he shouted: *"Tfû 'aleykum!"*† and spat upon the ground. No other word did he vouchsafe to them, but walked away; and he continued walking till he reached his native home. There, sitting in his ancient seat, he told his wife:

'"Take comfort, O beloved! I have found one filthier."'

Suleymân declared the story finished.

'Is there a moral to it?' asked Rashîd.

'The moral is self-evident,' replied the story-teller. 'It is this: however bad the woman whom one happens to possess may be, be certain it is always possible to find a worse.'

'It is also possible to find a better,' I suggested.

'Be not so sure of that!' said Suleymân. 'There are three several kinds of women in the world, who all make claim to be descended from our father Noah. But the truth is this: Our father Noah had one daughter only, and three men desired her; so not to disappoint the other two, he turned his donkey and his dog into two girls, whom he

† An insult.

34

presented to them, and that accounts for the three kinds of women now to be observed. The true descendants of our father Noah are very rare.'

'How may one know them from the others?' I inquired.

'By one thing only. They will keep your secret. The second sort of woman will reveal your secret to a friend; the third will make of it a tale against you. And this they do instinctively, as dogs will bark or asses bray, without malevolence or any kind of forethought.

'That same priest of the Maronites of whom I told just now, in the first days of his married life was plagued by his companion to reveal to her the secrets people told him in confession. He refused, declaring that she would divulge them.

'"Nay, I can keep a secret if I swear to do so. Only try me!" she replied.

'"Well, we shall see," the priest made answer, in a teasing manner.

'One day, as he reclined upon the sofa in their house, that priest began to moan and writhe as if in agony. His wife, in great alarm, inquired what ailed him.

'"It is a secret," he replied, "which I dare not confide to you , for with it is bound up my earthly welfare and my soul's salvation."

'"I swear by Allah I will hide it. Tell me!" she implored.

'"Well," he replied, as if in torment, "I will risk my life and trust you. Know you are in the presence of the greatest miracle. I, though not a woman, am far gone with child—a thing which never happened on the earth till now—and in this hour it is decreed that I produce my first-born."

'Then, with a terrific cry, he thrust his hand beneath his

petticoat, and showed his wife a little bird which he had kept there hidden. He let it fly away out through the window. Having watched it disappear, he said devoutly:

"'Praise be to Allah! That is over! You have seen my child. This is a sacred and an awful mystery. Preserve the secret, or we all are dead!'

"'I swear I will preserve it,' she replied, with fervour.

'But the miracle which she had witnessed burned her spirit. She knew that she must speak of it or die; and so she called upon a friend whose prudence she could trust, and binding her by vows, told her the story.

'This woman also had a trusted friend, to whom she told the story, under vows of secrecy, and so on, with the consequence that that same evening the priest received a deputation of the village elders, who requested, in the name of the community, to be allowed to kiss the feet of his mysterious son—that little, rainbow-coloured bird, which had a horn upon its head and played the flute.

'The priest said nothing to his wife. He did not beat her. He gave her but one look. And yet from that day forward, she never plagued him anymore, but was submissive.'

'The priest was wise on that occasion, yet so foolish in the other story!' I objected.

'The way of the majority of men!' said Suleymân. 'But women are more uniformly wise or foolish. A happy night!' said Suleymân conclusively, settling himself to sleep.

The usual night-light of the Syrian peasants—a wick afloat upon a saucerful of oil and water—burned upon the ground between us, making great shadows dance upon the walls and vaulting. The last I heard before I fell asleep was Rashîd's voice, exclaiming:

'He is a famous liar, is our wise man yonder; yet he speaks the truth!'

THE SACK WHICH CLANKED

The sand which had been a rich ochre turned to creamy white, the sea from blue became a livid green, the grass upon the sand-hills blackened and bowed down beneath a sudden gust of wind. The change was instantaneous, as it seemed to me. I had observed that clouds were gathering upon the mountain peaks inland, but I had been riding in hot sunlight, only a little less intense than it had been at noon, when suddenly the chill and shadow struck me. Then I saw the sky completely overcast with a huge purple cloud which bellied down upon the land and sea. The waves which had been lisping all day long gave forth an ominous dull roar. White horses reared and plunged. A wind sang through the grass and thistles of the dunes, driving the sand into my face.

Rashîd, who had been riding far behind, in conversation with our muleteer, came tearing up, and I could hear the shouts of the *mukâri* urging his two beasts to hurry.

'There is a village on the headland over there—a village of Circassian settlers,' cried my servant, breathless. 'It has a bad name, and I had not thought to spend the night there. But any roof is good in such a storm. Ride fast! We may arrive before the downpour.'

My horse had broken to a canter of his own accord. I urged him to a gallop. We flew round the bay. The village on the headland took shape rapidly—a few cube-shaped, whitewashed houses perched amid what seemed at first to be great rocks, but on a close approach revealed themselves as blocks of masonry, the ruins of some city of antiquity. From time to time a jet of spray shot up above them, white as lilies in the gloom. The sea was rising. I discerned an ancient gateway opening on the beach, and set my horse towards it, while the rain came down in sheets. I saw no more until the ruins loomed up close before me, a blind wall.

'Your right hand!' called Rashîd; and, bearing to the right, I found the gateway. We waited underneath its vault until the muleteer, a dripping object, shrouded in a sack, came up with his two mules; and then we once more plunged into the deluge. The path, a very rough one, wavered up and down and in and out among the ruins. There were, perhaps, a dozen scattered houses without gardens or any sign of cultivation round them. Only one of them possessed an upper storey, and towards that, supposing it to be the guest-room, we now picked our way. It stood alone right out upon the promontory, topped by clouds of spray.

A little courtyard gave us partial shelter while Rashîd ran up some rough stone steps and hammered at a door, exclaiming:

'Peace be on this house! My master craves for food and shelter, and we, his servants, ask the same boon of your goodness. O master of the house, God will reward your hospitality!'

The door was opened and a man appeared, bidding us all come in, in Allah's name. He was of middle height and thick-set, with a heavy grey moustache. An old-fashioned, low-crowned fez, with large blue tassel, was bound about his brow with an embroidered turban. A blue zouave jacket, crimson vest and baggy trousers of a darker blue completed his apparel, for his feet were bare. In his girdle were a pair of pistols and a scimitar.

He bade us welcome in bad Arabic, showing us into a good-sized room—the upper chamber we had seen from far. Its windows, innocent of glass, were closed by wooden shutters, roughly bolted, which creaked and rattled in the gale. A very fine-looking old man rose from the divan to greet us.

'What countryman are you? A Turk, or one of us?' he asked, as I removed my head-shawl. 'An Englishman, say you?' He seized my hand, and pressed it. 'An Englishman—any Englishman—is good, and his word is sure. But the English Government is very bad. Three Englishmen in Kars behaved like warrior-angels, fought like devils. And while they fought for us their Government betrayed our country. What? You have heard about it? Praise to Allah! At last I meet with one who can confirm the story. My son here thinks that I invented it.'

I happened to have read of the defence of Kars under the leadership of three heroic Englishmen—General Williams, Captain Teesdale, and Doctor Sandwith—and of the betrayal of the Circassian rising under Shamyl at the time of the Crimean war.

The old man was delighted. 'Listen, O my son!' he called out to the person who had let us in. 'It is true what I have often told to you . This Englishman knows all about it. So does all the world, except such blockheads as yourself and your companions.'

His son begged to be excused a minute while he put his crops into the barn. Therewith he dragged a sack out of the room. What crops he may have grown I do not know; but this I know—the contents of that sack clanked as he dragged it out.

When he returned, he brought a bowl of eggs cooked in clarified butter, two slabs of bread, and a great jug of water, apologising for the coarseness of the fare. We all supped together, the old man babbling of the days of old with great excitement. His son stared at me with unblinking eyes. At last he said:

'I like you , O *khawâjah*. I had once a son about your age. Say, O my father, is there not a strong resemblance?'

Thereafter he talked quite as much as the old man, giving me the history of their emigration from the Caucasus to escape the yoke of the accursed Muscovite, and enumerating all the troubles which attended their first coming into Syria.

'We are not subjects of the Government,' he told me, 'but allies; and we have special privileges. But the dishonoured dogs round here forget old compacts, and want us to pay taxes like mere *fellâhîn*.'

We sat up talking far into the night, while the storm raged without, and the rain and the sea-spray pounded on the shutters; and never have I met with kinder treatment. It was the custom for chance comers to have food at evening only and leave betimes next morning. But our host, when I awoke in splendid sunlight, had breakfast ready—sour milk and Arab bread and fragrant coffee—and when I went out to my horse he followed me, and thrust two roasted fowls into my saddle-bags, exclaiming '*Zâd!*'—which means 'food for the road.' And much to my abashment he and the old man fell upon my neck and kissed me on both cheeks.

'Good people! The very best of people! They would take no money. God reward them,' chanted Rashîd, as we rode out of the ruins inland through a garden of wild flowers. The storm had passed completely. Not a cloud remained.

After an hour we came in sight of a large *khan* outside a mud-built village on the shore. Before it was a crowd, including several soldiers. As we drew near, Rashîd inquired the meaning of the throng.

'A great calamity,' he was informed. 'A man, a foreigner, is dying, killed by highwaymen. One of his companions, a poor servant, is already dead.'

We both dismounted, and Rashîd pushed in to learn more of the matter. Presently a soldier came to me.

'Your Honour is an Englishman?' he questioned. 'Praise be to Allah! I am much relieved. This other also is an Englishman, they tell me. He is severely wounded, at the gate of death.'

I went with him at once to see the sufferer, who seemed relieved to hear me speak, but could not answer. Rashîd and I did what we could to make him comfortable, giving the soldiers orders to keep out the crowd. We decided to ride on and send a doctor, and then report the matter to a British consul.

'He was going down to start some kind of business in the city over there,' the leader of the soldiers told me, nodding towards the south. 'He had a largish company, with several camels. But near the village of —— he was attacked by the Circassians, and was so foolish as to make resistance. They took everything he had of worth—his arms, his money—and killed a camel-driver, besides wounding him. It happened yesterday before the storm. They say I should take vengeance for him. What am I—a corporal with six men—to strive with Huseyn Agha and his cavalry! It needs a regiment.'

He went grumbling off. Rashîd and I were staring hard at one another; for the village named was that where we had spent the night, and Huseyn Agha's roasted fowls were in our saddle-bags.

Rashîd, as I could see, was troubled upon my account. He kept silence a good while. At last he said:

'It is like this, my lord. Each man must see with his own eyes and not another's. People are as one finds them, good or bad. They change with each man's vision, yet remain the same. For us those highway robbers are good people; we must bless them; having cause to do so. This other man is free to curse them, if he will. Good to their friends, bad to their enemies. What creature of the sons of Adam can condemn them quite?'

POLICE WORK

Having to dress for dinner on a certain evening, I took off my money-belt, and quite forgot to put it on again. It happened to contain twelve English pounds. I left it lying on the table in the hotel bedroom. When I came back in the small hours of the morning it was gone. Rashîd—who slept out at a *khan* in charge of our two horses—came in at eight o'clock to rouse me. Hearing of my loss, he gave me the worst scolding I have ever had, and then went out to blow up the hotel proprietor.

It was, for once, a real hotel with table d'hôte, hall-porter, and a palm-lounge—everything, in fact, excepting drains. The owner was a fat, brown individual, whom I had generally seen recumbent on a sofa in his office, while someone of his many sons did all the work. But that he could show energy upon occasion I now learnt. Hearing from Rashîd that I, a guest in his hotel, had suffered robbery, he sprang on to his feet and danced with rage.

When I arrived upon the scene, which was the palm-lounge—an open courtyard shaded by an awning—he was flourishing a monstrous whip, with dreadful imprecations, literally foaming at the mouth. I begged him to do nothing rash, but he seemed not to hear me. With the squeal of a fighting stallion, he rushed off to the servants' quarters, whence presently there came heartrending shrieks and cries for mercy. His sons, in fear of murder, followed him, and added their remonstrance to the general din. The women of his house appeared in doorways, weeping and wringing their hands.

Rashîd seemed gratified by this confusion, regarded as a tribute to our greatness, his and mine.

'Be good enough to go away,' he told me. 'The scene is quite unworthy of your dignity. I will take care that all is done to raise your honour.'

I remained, however. Presently, the host returned, perspiring freely, mopping his brown face with a crimson handkerchief. He smiled as one who has had healthy exercise.

'It is no use,' he told me, with a shrug. 'I beat them well, and every one of them confessed that he alone, and not another, was the thief. Each, as his turn came, wished to stay my hand at any cost.'

He sank down on a sofa which was in the court. 'What further is your Honour's will?' he asked. 'I will beat anyone. The story is so bad for the hotel. I should be ruined if it reached the ears of Cook or Baedeker.'

The cries of those unhappy servants having shamed me, I told him that I was content to count the money lost rather than that harmless folk should suffer for my carelessness. Rashîd protested, saying twelve pounds was no trifle, although I might, in youthful folly, so regard it. He, as my servant, had to guard my wealth.

'The gold is lost. It is the will of Allah. Let it be,' I answered irritably.

'You will not tell the English consul?' cried the host, with sudden eagerness. 'You will refrain from saying any word to Cook or Baedeker to bring ill-fame and ruin on the place? Our Lord augment your wealth and guard you always! May your progeny increase in honour till it rules the world!'

'But something must be done,' Rashîd remonstrated. 'A crime has been committed. We must find the culprit.'

'True,' said the host, 'and I will help with all my strength. The consul would not help at all. He would but frighten the police, with the result that they would torture—perhaps hang—a man or two, but not the man who stole your belt of money. Our police, when not alarmed, are clever. Go to them and give a little money. They will find the thief.'

'I go this minute,' said Rashîd.

I bade him wait. Knowing his way of magnifying me and my possessions, I thought it better to be present at the interview, lest he should frighten the police no less than would the intervention of a consul.

We went together through the shady markets, crossing here and there an open space of blinding sunlight, asking our way at intervals, until at last we entered a large whitewashed room where soldiers loitered and a frock-coated, be-fezzed official sat writing at a desk. This personage was very sympathetic.

'Twelve pounds!' he cried. 'It is a serious sum. The first thing to be done is to survey the scene of crime. Wait, I will send with you a knowing man.'

He called one of the soldiers, who stepped forward and saluted, and gave him charge of the affair.

'You can place confidence in him. He knows his business,' he assured me, bowing with extreme politeness, as we took our leave.

With the soldier who had been assigned to us we sauntered back to the hotel. The man abounded in compassion for me. He said it was the worst case he had ever heard of—to rob a man so manifestly good and amiable of so great a sum. Alas! the badness of some people. It put out the sun!

At the hotel he spent a long while in my room, searching,

as he said, for 'traces.' Rashîd, the host and all his family, and nearly all the servants, thronged the doorway. After looking into every drawer, and crawling underneath the bed, which he unmade completely, he spent some minutes in debating whether the thief had entered by the window or the door. Having at last decided for the door, he turned to me and asked if there was anybody I suspected. When I answered 'no,' I saw him throw a side-glance at Rashîd, as if he thought him fortunate in having so obtuse a master. As he was departing, Rashîd, at my command, gave him a silver coin, for which he kissed my hand and, having done so, said:

'I know a clever man, none like him for such business. I will send him to your presence in an hour.'

Three hours passed. I had finished luncheon, and was sipping coffee in the lounge, when a sleek personage in gorgeous robes was brought to me. He had a trick of looking down his nose at his moustache, the while he stroked it, with a gentle smirk.

'Your Excellency has been robbed,' he murmured in a secret tone, 'and you would know the robber? There is nothing simpler. I have discovered many thieves. I think it likely that I know the very man. I will disguise myself as an old woman or a begging dervish. There are many ways. But, first, your Honour must bestow on me an English pound. That is my fee. It is but little for such services.'

I answered languidly that the affair had ceased to thrill me; I wished to hear no more about the money or the thief. He stayed a long while, wheedling and remonstrating, depicting his own subtlety in glowing terms; but in the end departed with despairing shrugs and backward glances, hoping that I might relent.

Rashîd, who had been out to tend the horses, came

presently and asked if I had seen the great detective. When I described our interview, he nearly wept.

'The people here think me the thief,' he told me. 'They say nothing, but I feel it in their bearing towards me. And now you give up seeking for the culprit! Am I to bear this shame for evermore?'

Here was a new dilemma! No way out of it appeared to me, for even if we did employ the great detective, our chance of finding the delinquent seemed exceeding small. I was thinking what could possibly be done to clear Rashîd, when a familiar figure came into the court and strolled towards us. It was Suleymân! I had imagined him three hundred miles away, at Gaza, in the south of Palestine. Loud were our exclamations, but his calm rebuked us. I never knew him show excitement or surprise.

He heard our story with deliberation, and shook his head at the police and the detective.

'No use at all,' he scoffed. 'The one man for your purpose is the Chief of the Thieves. I know him intimately.'

'*Ma sh'Allah!* Is there then a guild of thieves?'

'There is.'

'The Sheykh of the Thieves must be the greatest rogue. I do not care to have to do with him.'

'You err,' remarked Suleymân, with dignity. 'Your error has its root in the conviction that a thief is evil. He may be evil as an individual; all men are apt to be who strive for gain; but as a member of a corporation he has pride and honour. With Europeans, it is just the opposite. They individually are more honourable than their governments and corporations. The Sheykh of the Thieves, I can assure you, is the soul of honour. I go at once to see him. He can clear Rashîd.'

'If he does that, he is the best of men!' exclaimed my servant.

An hour later one of the hotel men, much excited, came to tell me that some soldiers were approaching, who had caught the thief. The host and all his family ran out into the hall. Rashîd and all the servants came from kitchen purlieus. Four soldiers entered with triumphant exclamations, dragging and pushing forward—Suleymân!

The prisoner's demeanour had its usual calm.

'I have regained the belt,' he called to me. 'These men were watching near the house, and found it on me. They would not hear reason. The man who stole the belt—a Greek—has left the city. He gave the Sheykh the belt, but kept the money.'

The soldiers, disappointed, let him go.

'How do you know all that?' inquired their leader.

'The Headman of the Thieves informed me of it.'

'Ah, then, it is the truth,' the soldier nodded. 'He is a man of honour. He would not deceive you.'

I do not claim to understand these things. I but relate them.

My Countryman

One summer, in the south of Syria, amid that tumbled wilderness of cliff and chasm, shale and boulder, which surges all around the Sea of Lot, we had been riding since the dawn without encountering a human being, and with relief at last espied a village, having some trace of cultivated land about it, and a tree.

Rashîd was on ahead. Suleymân had been beside me, but had dropped behind in order to perform some operation on his horse's hoof. As I came down the last incline on to the village level I heard angry shouts, and saw a crowd of *fellâhîn* on foot mobbing Rashîd. Urging my horse, I shouted to him to know what was happening. At once a number of the villagers forsook him and surrounded me, waving their arms about and talking volubly.

I had gathered, from their iteration of the one word '*moyeh*,' that water was the matter in dispute, even before Rashîd succeeded in rejoining me.

He said: 'I rode up to the spring which flows beneath that arch, and was letting my horse drink from the stone trough of water, when these maniacs rushed up and dragged my horse away, and made this noise. They say the water in the spring is theirs, and no one else has any right to touch it. I offered to make payment, but they would not hear me. I threatened them with vengeance, but they showed no fear. Is it your Honour's will that I should beat a few of them?'

Seeing their numbers, I considered it the wiser plan for

us to let them be till their excitement had cooled down, and till Suleymân arrived to help us with advice. Accordingly, I smiled and nodded to the villagers, and rode back up the path a little way, Rashîd obeying my example with reluctance, muttering curses on their faith and ancestry. Then we dismounted and lay down in the shadow of some rocks. It wanted still two hours before the sun would set.

Suleymân came on us, and dismounted at a call from me.

'What is the noise down there?' he questioned, looking at the village with that coolness, like indifference, habitual to his face when meeting problems of importance.

'They will not let us touch the water—curse their fathers!' growled Rashîd. 'Heard anyone the like of such inhospitality? It would but serve them right if we destroyed their houses.'

Suleymân screwed up his eyes, the better to survey the crowd of villagers below, who now sat guard around the spring, and murmured carelessly:

'It is evident that you have angered them, O son of rashness. We shall do well to wait before approaching them again with our polite request.'

Therewith he stretched his length upon the ground, with a luxurious sigh, and would, I think, have gone to sleep, had not Rashîd, conceiving himself blamed, thought necessary to relate in full the whole adventure.

'What else could man have done?' he asked defiantly. 'Say in what respect, however trifling, did I act unwisely?'

'By Allah, you did nothing wrong, and yet you might have done better, since your efforts led to failure,' said the sage, benignly. 'You are a soldier yet in thought, and your one method is to threaten. If that avails not, you are helpless. There are other ways.'

'I offered money,' cried Rashîd indignantly. 'Could man do more?'

'What are those other ways? Instruct us, O beloved!' I put in, to save Rashîd from feeling lonely under blame for ignorance.

'No truly great one ever argues with a crowd. He chooses out one man, and speaks to him, him only,' said Suleymân; and he was going to tell us more, but just then something in the *wadi* down below the village caught his eye, and he sat up, forgetting our dilemma.

'A marvel!' he exclaimed after a moment spent in gazing. 'Never, I suppose, since first this village was created, have two Franks approached it in a single day before. you are as one of us in outward seeming,' he remarked to me; 'but yonder comes a perfect Frank with two attendants.'

We looked in the direction which his finger pointed, and beheld a man on horseback clad in white from head to foot, with a pith helmet and a puggaree, followed by two native servants leading sumpter-mules.

'Our horses are in need of water,' growled Rashîd, uninterested in the sight. 'It is a sin for those low people to refuse it to us.'

'Let us first wait and see how this newcomer fares, what method he adopts,' replied Suleymân, reclining once more at his ease.

The Frank and his attendants reached the outskirts of the village, and headed naturally for the spring. The *fellâhîn*, already put upon their guard by Rashîd's venture, opposed them in a solid mass. The Frank expostulated. We could hear his voice of high command.

'Aha, he knows some Arabic. He is a missionary, not a traveller,' said Suleymân, who now sat up and showed keen interest. 'I might have known it, for the touring season is long past.'

He rose with dignified deliberation and remounted. We followed him as he rode slowly down towards the scene of strife. When we arrived, the Frank, after laying about him vainly with his riding-whip, had drawn out a revolver. He was being stoned. His muleteers had fled to a safe distance. In another minute, as it seemed, he would have shot some person, when nothing under Allah could have saved his life.

Suleymân cried out in English: 'Don't you be a fool, sir! Don't you fire!'

The Frank looked round in our direction, with an angry face; but Suleymân bestowed no further thought on him. He rode up to the nearest group of *fellâhîn*, crying aloud:

'O true believers! O asserters of the Unity! Bless the Prophet, and inform me straightway what has happened!'

Having captured their attention by this solemn adjuration, he inquired:

'Who is the chief among you? Let him speak, him only!'

Although the crowd had seemed till then to be without a leader, an old white-bearded man was thrust before him, with the cry:

'Behold our Sheykh, O lord of judgment. Question him!'

Rashîd and I heard nothing of the conversation which ensued, except the tone of the two voices, which appeared quite friendly, and some mighty bursts of laughter from the crowd. No more stones were thrown, although some persons still kept guard over the spring.

At length Suleymân returned to us, exclaiming:

'All is well. They grant us leave to take what water we require. The spring has been a trouble to these people

53

through the ages because the wandering tribes with all their herds come here in time of drought and drink it dry. But now they are our friends, and make us welcome.'

He called out to the Frank, who all this while had sat his horse with an indignant air, more angry, as it seemed, to be forgotten than to be assailed:

'It is all right. You take the water and you pay them five *piastres*.'

'It is extortion!' cried the Frank. 'What right have they to charge me money for the water of this natural spring, which is the gift of God? I will not pay.'

'No matter. I pay for you,' shrugged Suleymân.

I tried to make the missionary—for such he proved to be upon acquaintance—understand that the conditions in that desert country made the spring a valued property, and gave a price to every pitcherful of water.

'What! Are you English?' was his only answer, as he scanned my semi-native garb with pity and disgust. 'And who, pray, is that person with you who was rude to me?'

'His name is Suleymân. He is a friend of mine.'

'A friend, I hardly think,' replied the Frank, fastidiously. He was a big man, with a dark complexion and light eyes. 'I am going to camp here tonight. I have a tent. Perhaps you will be good enough to come and sup with me. Then we can talk.'

'With pleasure,' I made answer, taken by surprise.

'Where is your camp?' he asked.

'We haven't got one. We put up in the guest-room if there is one, or under the stars.'

'Well, there's no accounting for tastes,' he murmured, with a sneer.

Rashîd, through all this conversation, had been standing by, waiting to tell me that Suleymân had gone before into the village to the headman's house, where it had been arranged that we should pass the night. Thither we went, when I had finished speaking to the missionary; and there we found Suleymân enthroned among the village elders in a long, low room. He stood up on my entrance, as did all the others, and explained:

'We have a room nearby where we can throw our saddle-bags, but it is verminous, and so we will not sleep inside it, but outside—on the roof. For supper we are the invited guests of the good sheykh, and I can tell you he is getting ready a fine feast.'

With deep regret and some degree of shame I told him of my promise to take supper with the missionary. He looked reproach at me, and told the villagers what I had said. They all cried out in disappointment. Suleymân suggested that I should revoke the promise instantly, but that I would not do, to his annoyance; and after that, till it was time for me to go, he and Rashîd were sulky and withdrew their eyes from me. I knew that they were jealous of the Frank, whom they regarded as an enemy, and feared lest he should turn my mind against them.

The Parting of the Ways

It was dusk when I set out for the missionary's tent, and starlit night before I reached it—so fleeting is the summer twilight in that land.

Rashîd went with me, as in duty bound, and insisted on remaining with the servants of the missionary by the cook's fire, although I told him to go back repeatedly, knowing how his mouth must water for the headman's feast. The dudgeon which he felt at my desertion made him determined not to let me out of sight, and called for the martyrdom of someone, even let that someone be himself.

The missionary called: 'Come in!' while I was still a good way off the tent. Entering, I found him stretched on a deck-chair, with hands behind his head. He did not rise upon my entrance, but just smiled and pointed to another chair beyond a little folding table laid for supper.

He spoke of the day's heat and the fatigues of travel and the flies; and asked me how I could endure to sleep in native hovels full of fleas and worse.

I told him that, by Suleymân's arrangement, we were to sleep upon the roof for safety. He sniffed.

I then related a discussion I had overheard between Rashîd and Suleymân as to the best way of defeating those domestic pests, thinking to make him laugh. Rashîd had spoken of the virtues of a certain shrub; but Suleymân declared the best specific was a new-born baby. This, if laid within a room for a short while, attracted every insect. The babe should then be carried out and dusted. The missionary did not even smile.

'The brutes!' he murmured. 'How can you, an Englishman, and apparently a man of education, bear their intimacy?'

They had their good points, I asserted—though, I fear, but lamely; for the robustness of his attitude impressed me, he being a man, presumably, of wide experience, and, what is more, a clergyman—the kind of man I had been taught to treat with some respect.

He said no more till we had finished supper, which consisted of sardines and corned beef and sliced pineapple, tomatoes and half-liquid butter out of tins, and some very stale European bread which he had brought with him. Confronted with such mummy food, I thought with longing of the good, fresh meal which I had left behind me at the headman's house. He may have guessed my thoughts, for he observed: 'I never touch their food. It is insanitary'—which I knew to be exactly what they said of his.

The man who waited on us seemed to move in fear, and was addressed by his employer very curtly.

After the supper there was tea, which, I confess, was welcome, and then the missionary put me through a kind of catechism. Finding out who I was, and that we had some friends in common, he frowned deeply. He had heard of my existence in the land, it seemed.

'What are you doing here at all?' he asked severely. 'At your age you should be at college or in training for some useful work.'

'I'm learning things,' I told him rather feebly.

His point of view, the point of view of all my countrymen, imposed itself on me as I sat there before him, deeply conscious of my youth and inexperience.

'What things?' he asked. And then his tongue was loosed. He gave me his opinion of the people of the country, and particularly of my two companions. He had summed them up at sight. They were two cunning rogues, whose only object was to fleece me. He told me stories about Englishmen who had been ruined in that very way through making friends with natives whom they thought devoted to them. One story ended in a horrid murder. He wanted me to have no more to do with them, and when he saw I was attached to them, begged me earnestly to treat them always as inferiors, to 'keep them in their place'; and this I promised, coward-like, to do, although I knew that, in the way he meant, it was not in me.

It seemed that he himself was travelling in these wild places in search of an old Greek inscription, mention of which he had discovered in some book. He half-persuaded me to bear him company.

'You are doing no good here, alone with such companions,' he said, as I at last departed. 'Think over my advice to you. Go back to England. Come with me for the next few days, and share my tents. Then come and stay with me in Jerusalem, and we can talk things over.' There was no doubt of the kindliness of his intention.

I thanked him, and strolled back toward the village in the starlight, Rashîd, who, at my first appearance, had detached himself from a small group which sat around the missionary's kitchen fire, stalking on before me with a lantern.

It seemed a wonder that the village dogs, which had made so great a noise on our arrival in the place so short a while before, now took no notice, seeming to recognise our steps as those of lawful inmates.

At the headman's house Suleymân still sat up talking with the village elders. He expressed a hope that I had much enjoyed myself, but with a hint of grievance which I noticed as a thing expected. Looking round upon those eager, friendly faces, I compared them with the cold face of the missionary, who suddenly appeared to me as a great bird of prey. I hated him instinctively, for he was like a schoolmaster; and yet his words had weight, for I was young to judge, and schoolmasters, though hateful, have a knack of being in the right.

At last we three went up on to the roof to sleep. We had lain down and said 'goodnight' to one another, when Suleymân remarked, as if soliloquising:

'Things will never be the same.'

'What do you mean?' I questioned crossly.

'That missionary has spoilt everything. He told you not to trust us, not to be so friendly with persons who are natives of this land, and therefore born inferior.'

I made no answer, and Suleymân went on:

'A man who journeys in the desert finds a guide among the desert people, and he who journeys on the sea trusts seamen. What allegations did he make? I pray you tell us!'

'He told me stories of his own experience.'

'His experience is not, never will be, yours. He is the enemy. A tiger, if one asked him to describe mankind, would doubtless say that they are masters of the guile which brings destruction, deserving only to be clawed to death. Question the pigeons of some mosque, upon the other hand, and they will swear by Allah men are lords of all benevolence.'

Rashîd broke in: 'His boys, with whom I talked, inform

me that he is devoid of all humanity. He never thanks them for their work, however perfect, nor has a word of blessing ever passed his lips. He frowns continually. How can he be the same as one like you who laughs and talks?'

We had all three sat up, unconsciously. And we continued sitting up, debating miserably under the great stars, hearing the jackals' voices answer one another from hill to hill both near and far, all through that night, drawing ever closer one to another as we approached an understanding.

'An Englishman such as that missionary,' said Suleymân, 'treats good and bad alike as enemies if they are not of his nation. He gives bare justice; which, in human life, is cruelty. He keeps a strict account with every man. We, when we love a man, keep no account. We never think of what is due to us or our position. And when we hate—may God forgive us!—it is just the same—save with the very best and coolest heads among us.'

'But you are cunning, and have not our code of honour,' I objected, with satirical intention, though the statement sounded brutal.

'Your Honour says so!' cried Rashîd, half weeping. 'No doubt you are referring to that theft in the hotel, of which you thought so little at the time that you would take no action. That was the doing of a Greek, as was established. Say, can you of your own experience of children of the Arabs say that one of us has ever robbed you of a small para, or wronged you seriously?'

'I cannot,' was my answer, after brief reflection. 'But the experience of other, older men must weigh with me.'

'Let other men judge people as they find them, and do you likewise,' said Suleymân.

'He urged me to give up this aimless wandering and go with him in search of an old Greek inscription, not far off.

Within four days he hopes to see El Cuds again; and thence he urged me to return to England.'

At that my two companions became silent and exceeding still, as if some paralysing fear hung over them. It was the hour immediately before the dawn, and life seemed hopeless. The missionary's voice seemed then to me the call of duty, yet every instinct in my blood was fierce against it.

'Your Honour will do what he pleases,' said my servant mournfully.

'The Lord preserve you ever!' sighed Suleymân, 'you are the leader of the party. Give command.'

A streak of light grew on the far horizon, enabling us to see the outlines of the rugged landscape. A half-awakened wild-bird cried among the rocks below us. And suddenly my mind grew clear. I cared no longer for the missionary's warning. I was content to face the dangers which those warnings threatened; to be contaminated, even ruined as an Englishman. The mischief, as I thought it, was already done. I knew that I could never truly think as did that missionary, nor hold myself superior to Eastern folk again. If that was to be reprobate, then I was finished.

'Saddle the horses. We will start at once,' I told Rashîd. 'Before the missionary is afoot—towards the East.'

For a moment he sat motionless, unable to believe his ears. Then suddenly he swooped and kissed my hand, exclaiming: 'Praise be to Allah!'

'Praise be to Allah!' echoed Suleymân, with vast relief. 'The tiger in you has not triumphed. We shall still know joy.'

'I resign myself to be the pigeon of the mosque,' I answered, laughing happily.

Five minutes later we were riding towards the dawn, beginning to grow red behind the heights of Moab.

The Knight Errant

We had left Damascus after noon the day before, and had spent the night at a great fortress-*khan*—the first of many on the pilgrims' road. We had been on our way an hour before Rashîd discovered that he had left a pair of saddle-bags behind him at the *khan*; and as those saddle-bags contained belongings of Suleymân, the latter went back with him to retrieve them. I rode on slowly, looking for a patch of shade. Except the *khan*, a square black object in the distance, there was nothing in my range of vision to project a shadow larger than a good-sized thistle. Between a faint blue wave of mountains on the one hand and a more imposing but far distant range upon the other, the vast plain rolled to the horizon in smooth waves.

I was ascending such an undulation at my horse's leisure when a cavalier appeared upon its summit—a figure straight out of the pages of some book of chivalry, with coloured mantle streaming to the breeze, and lance held upright in the stirrup-socket. This knight was riding at his ease till he caught sight of me, when, with a shout, he laid his lance in rest, lowered his crest and charged. I was exceedingly alarmed, having no skill in tournament, and yet I could not bring myself to turn and flee. I rode on as before, though with a beating heart, my purpose, if I had one, being, when the moment came, to lean aside, and try to catch his spear, trusting in Allah that my horse would stand the shock. But the prospect of success was small, because I could see nothing clearly, till suddenly the thunder of the hoof-beats ceased, and I beheld the knight within ten yards of me, grinning and saluting me with lance erect, his horse flung back upon its haunches.

'I frightened you ,*O Faranji?*' he asserted mockingly.

I replied that it would take more than such a wretched mountebank as he could do to frighten me, and showed him my revolver, which, until the fear was over, had escaped my memory. It pleased him, and he asked for it immediately. I put it back.

'A pretty weapon,' he agreed, 'but still I frightened you.'

I shrugged and sneered, disdaining further argument, and thought to pass him; but he turned his horse and rode beside me, asking who I was and where I came from, and what might be my earthly object in riding thus towards the desert all alone. I answered all his questions very coldly, which did not disconcert him in the least. Hearing that I had attendants, one of whom had skill in warfare, he said that he would wait with me till they came up. I tried to frighten him with tales of all the men Rashîd had slain in single combat: he was all the more determined to remain with me, saying that he would gain much honour from destroying such a man.

'But I do suspect that you are lying, O most noble *Faranji*, and that this boasted champion is some wretched townsman whose only courage is behind a wall,' he chuckled.

At that I was indignant, and I lied the more.

Thus talking, we came near a piece of ruined wall, which cast sufficient shadow for a man to rest in. The knight dismounted and tied up his horse. I was for riding on, but he made such an outcry that, wishing to avoid a quarrel, I alighted also and tied up my horse. We lay down near together in the strip of shade. He passed me a rough leathern water-bottle, and I took a draught of warmish fluid, tasting like the smell of goats. He took a longer draught, and then exclaimed: 'There are your friends.'

Far off upon the plain two specks were moving. I could not have told man from man at such a distance, but the knight was able to distinguish and describe them accurately.

'The younger man who sits erect upon his horse—he is no doubt the warrior of whom you speak. The other, plump and lolling, has the air of greatness—a *Pasha*, maybe, or a man of law.'

I told him that Suleymân was a man of learning, and then let him talk while I took stock of his appearance. The figure out of books of chivalry was shabby on a close inspection. The coloured surcoat was both weather-stained and torn, the coat of mail beneath so ancient that many of the links had disappeared completely; the holes where they had been were patched with hide, which also was beginning to give way in places. His age was about three-and-twenty; he had bright brown eyes, a black moustache and beard, and a malicious air. He looked a perfect ragamuffin, yet he spoke with condescension, talking much about his pedigree, which contained a host of names which I had never heard before—a fact which, when he realised it, filled him first with horror, then with pity of my ignorance. He expatiated also on his horse's pedigree, which was as lengthy as his own.

When my friends came up, I quite expected them to rid me of the tiresome knight. But they did nothing of the sort. They took the man and his pretensions seriously, exchanging with him compliments in striking contrast with the haughty tone I had till then adopted. Rashîd refused his challenge with politeness, and, much to my dismay,

Suleymân, the older and more thoughtful man, accepted it upon condition that the combat should stand over till some more convenient time; and when the knight proclaimed his sovereign will to travel with us, they seemed pleased.

'He will be useful to us,' said Rashîd, when I complained to him of this deception, 'for his tribe controls a great part of this country. But it will be best for me to carry our revolver while he rides with us. Then I and not your Honour can deny him, which is more becoming.'

The knight had asked for my revolver thrice already.

That evening, near a lonely village of the plain, the battle with Suleymân was fought with equal honours, each rider hitting his man squarely with the long *jerideh*—the stripped palm-branch—which is substituted for the spear in friendly combat. The heroes faced each other at a regulated distance. Then one—it was Suleymân—clapped spurs into his horse's flanks and fled, keeping within a certain space which might be called the lists; the other flying after him, with fearful yells, intent to fling the missile so that it should strike the victim in a certain manner. This lasted till the throw was made, and then the order was reversed, and the pursuer in his turn became the hunted.

The knight applauded his opponent's skill reluctantly, and with regret that he himself had not been in his usual form.

He journeyed with us after that for many days. It seemed that he was out in search of exploits, so did not care a jot which way he rode. In former days, he told me, there used to be a tournament in every town each Friday, where any stranger knight might show his prowess, winning honour and renown. But in these degenerate times it was necessary for the would-be champion to cry his challenge in some public place, or else arrange the fight beforehand meanly in some tavern. I should have been delighted with him on the whole, if he had not been quarrelsome and had not expected us, as his companions, to extricate him from the strife in which his arrogance involved him. We dreaded the arrival at a town or village. If he had possessed the prowess of his courage, which was absolutely reckless, he would have been a more endurable, if dread, companion. But in almost every quarrel which he brought upon himself he got the worst of it, and was severely beaten, and then would talk to us about the honour of the Arabs till we fell asleep.

One night in the small town of Mazarib we rescued him from two Circassian bravoes whom he had insulted wantonly. They had nearly stopped his mouth forever when we intervened. I cannot say he was ungrateful upon that occasion. On the contrary, he swore that he would not forsake us until death—a vow which filled us with dismay, for even Suleymân by that time saw that he was useless; and Rashîd, our treasurer, resented his contempt of money. He had a way, too, of demanding anything of ours which took his fancy, and, if not forcibly prevented, taking it, peculiarly obnoxious to Rashîd, who idolised my few belongings. We were his friends, his manner told us, and he, the bravest of the brave, the noblest of the noble Arabs, was prepared to give his life for us at any time. Any trifles therefore which we might bestow on him were really nothing as compared with what he gave us every hour of every day.

It grew unbearable. The people in the *khan* at Mazarib were laughing at us because that wretched *Bedawi*, a chance adherent, ruled our party. We plotted desperately to get rid of him.

At length Suleymân devised a scheme. It was that we should change the whole direction of our journey, turning aside into the mountain of the *Druzes*. The *Druzes* were at war with many of the *Bedu*—probably with this man's tribe; at any rate, a *Bedawi*, unless disguised, would run grave risk among them while the war was on.

Accordingly, when we at length set out from Mazarib, Suleymân, with many compliments, informed the knight of a dilemma which distressed us greatly. I had been summoned to the bedside of a friend of mine, a great *Druze sheykh*, now lying very ill, whose one wish was to gaze on me before he died. Rashîd chimed in to say how tenderly that *Druze* chief loved me, and how depressed I was by sorrow for his grievous illness. In short, it was imperative that we should go at once to the *Druze* mountain. What were our feelings when we suddenly bethought us that there was danger in that region for an Arab knight! Must we then part from our beloved, from our souls' companion? Suleymân declared that we had wept like babes at such a prospect. No, that must never be; our grief would kill us. We had been obliged to think of some contrivance by which our hearts' delight might bear us company without much risk, and with the help of Allah we had hit upon a splendid plan, yet simple: That he should lay aside his lance and armour, dress as a Christian, and become our cook.

'Why need he seem a Christian?' asked Rashîd.

'Because all cooks who go with English travellers are Christians,' was the earnest answer, 'and because no man would ever think to find a *Bedawi* beneath a Christian's cloak.'

'A person of my master's standing ought to have a cook,' murmured Rashîd, as one who thought aloud.

Never have I seen such horror in the face of man as then convulsed the features of the desert knight. He, a cook!

He, the descendant of I know not whom, to wear the semblance of a heathen and degraded townsman! Rather than that he would encounter twenty spear-points. If we were going to the mountain of the *Druzes*, we might go alone!

We all were eager to express regret. He listened with a sneer, and answered nothing. After a while he beckoned me to speak apart with him, and, when we were beyond the hearing of the others, said:

'I leave you now, O *Faranji*, and journey towards Nejd to seek adventures. You love me I am aware, and so I grieve to part from you; but your adherents are low people and devoured by envy. If ever we should meet again I will destroy them. If you should travel south and eastward through the Belka, remember me, I beg, and seek our tents. There you shall find a welcome far more hospitable than the *Druze* will give you. I shall never cease to pray for you. My grief will be extreme until we meet again. I pray you give me that revolver as a souvenir.'

THE FANATIC

A European hat in those days was a rarity except in the large towns, and it attracted notice. That is the reason why I generally discarded it, with other too conspicuously Western adjuncts. Where the inhabitants were not well-mannered, the hat was apt to be saluted with a shower of stones.

One afternoon I happened to be riding by myself along a so-called road in the bare mountain country round Jerusalem, wearing a hat, when I came on a pedestrian resting in the shadow of a rock by the wayside. He was a native Christian—that much could be detected at a glance; but of what peculiar brand I could not guess from his costume, which consisted of a *fez*, a clerical black coat and waistcoat, quite of English cut, but very much the worse for wear; a yellow flannel shirt, and a red cord with tassels worn by way of necktie; baggy Turkish pantaloons; white stockings, and elastic-sided boots. Beside him, a long staff leaned up against the rock. He sprang upon his feet at my approach, and, with an amiable smile and bow, exclaimed:

'Good afternoon. I think you are an English gentleman?'

I pleaded guilty to the charge, and he asked leave to walk beside me until past a certain village, not far distant, of which the people, he assured me, were extremely wicked and averse to Christians. I readily consented, and he took his staff and walked beside me, pouring out his soul in fulsome flattery.

The village which he dreaded to approach alone was the

abode of Muslims, devilish people who hate the righteous Christians and persecute them when they get the chance. He said that he looked forward to the day when the English would take over the whole country and put those evil-doers in their proper place, below the Christians. It would be a mercy and a blessing to the human race, he gave as his mature opinion, if the English were to conquer the whole world. They were so good and upright and so truly pious. He did not think that any wrong was ever done in England. And then:

'You are a Brûtestant?' he asked.

I answered that I was a member of the Church of England.

'Ah, thank God!' he cried. 'I also am a Brûtestant—a Babtist.' He seemed to think that my avowal made us brothers.

It seemed, from the account he gave me of himself, that he was an evangelist, working to spread the truth among his wicked country-people; for the Christians of the Greek and Latin Churches were both wicked and benighted, he informed me, and would persecute him, like the Muslims, if they got the chance. It was hard work, he told me, turning up his eyes to heaven. He grieved to say it, but there seemed no other way to purge the land of all those wicked people save destruction. He wondered that the Lord had not destroyed them long ago. Yet when I said that I did not agree with him, but thought that they were decent folk, though rather backward, he came round to my opinion in a trice, exclaiming:

'Ah, how true you speak! It is that they are backward. They will neffer be no better till they get the Gosbel light, the liffin water.'

I told him he was talking nonsense; that, for my part, I

thought the missionaries did more harm than good, and once again he changed his standpoint, though less boldly, saying:

'It is so delightful to talk thus freely to a noble English gentleman. God knows that I could listen for a day without fatigue, you talk so sweet. And what you say is all so new to me.'

And he proceeded to relate with what severity the English missionaries treated native converts like himself, mentioning many wicked things which they had done in his remembrance. I could not but admire his versatility and total lack of shame in his desire to please. Thus talking, we approached the village of his fears.

'If I was by myself I should be much afraid,' he fawned; 'but not with you. These wicked beoble do not dare to hurt an English gentleman, who wears the hat and is brotected by the Bowers of Eurobe.'

We had not really got into the place before some boys at play among the rocks outside the houses, spying my hat, threw stones in our direction. One hit my horse. I raised my whip and rode at them. They fled with screams of terror. Glancing back, I could perceive no sign of my devout companion. But when I returned at leisure, having driven the young rogues to cover, I found him vigorously beating a small boy who had fallen in the panic flight and, finding himself left behind, had been too frightened to get up again.

Never have I seen a face of such triumphant malice as then appeared on that demure evangelist. He beat the child as if he meant to kill it, muttering execrations all the while and looking round him furtively for fear lest other Muslims should appear in sight, in which case, I believe, he would at once have turned from blows to fondling.

'The wicked boy!' he cried, as I came up, 'to throw stones at a noble English gentleman. He well deserfs to be deliffered ofer to the Bowers of Eurobe.'

I bade him leave the child alone, or it would be the worse for him. Aggrieved, and, in appearance, shocked at my unsympathetic tone, he left his prey, and I endeavoured to speak comfort to the victim; who, however, took no notice of my words, but ran hard for the village, howling lustily.

'The wicked boy! The wicked children!' the evangelist kept moaning, in hesitating and half-contrite tones. 'It is a bity that you let him go. He will perhabs make trouble for us in the fillage. But you are so brafe. I think the English are the brafest kind of beeble.'

I also thought it possible there might be trouble; but I decided to go on, not wishing to show fear before that craven. He cried aloud in awe and wonder when I told him that little boys threw stones in Christian England.

'But only upon unbelievers!' he exclaimed imploringly, as one who would preserve his last illusion.

I replied to the effect that members of the Church of England would, no doubt, have stoned a Baptist or a Roman Catholic with pleasure, if such heretics with us had dressed in a peculiar way; but that, in my opinion, it was only natural instinct in a boy to throw a stone at any living thing which seemed unusual.

The shock this information gave him—or his private terrors—kept him silent through the village; where the people, men and women, watched us pass with what appeared to be unfriendly faces. I was ill at ease, expecting some attack at every step.

As luck would have it, at the far end of the place, when I could see the open country, and was giving thanks for our escape, a great big stone was thrown by a small boy quite close to me. It struck me on the arm, and hurt enough to make me really angry.

'For God's sake, sir!' implored my terrified companion, 'Ride on! Do nothing! There are men obserfing.'

I heard him taking to his heels. But I had caught the culprit, and was beating him. His yells went forth with terrible insistence:

'O my father, O my mother, help. Ya Muslimin!'

And, in a trice, I was surrounded by a group of surly-looking *fellâhîn*, one of whom told me curtly to release the boy. I did so instantly, prepared for trouble. But no sooner had I left off beating than that man began. The boy's appeals for help went forth anew; but this time he addressed them to his mother only, for his father held him.

I begged the man to stop, and in the end he did so.

All those ferocious-looking *fellâhîn* returned my smile at this conclusion, and wished me a good evening as I rode away.

I never saw that bright evangelist again. No doubt he ran till he had reached some place inhabited by altogether righteous Christian people. But the way he started running was a clear inducement to pursuit to any son of Adam not evangelised.

RASHÎD'S REVENGE

We were staying with an English friend of mine—a parson, though the least parsonical of men—who had a pleasant little house in a *Druze* village of Mount Lebanon, and nothing to do but watch, and do his utmost to restrain, the antics of a very wealthy and eccentric lady missionary. He had gone away for a few weeks, leaving us in possession, when another sort of clergyman arrived—a little man with long white beard, sharp nose, and pale, seraphic eyes. He was, or fancied that he was, on duty, inspecting missionary establishments in those mountains. The master of the house had once invited him to stay there if he passed that way. He seemed surprised to find us in possession, and treated us as interlopers, though I was in fact his host, regarding our small dwelling as a clergy house. His gaze expressed an innocent surprise when I sat down to supper with him and performed the honours on the night of his arrival. He gave his orders boldly to my servant, and his demeanour plainly asked what business I had there, though he would never listen to my explanation.

I took the whole adventure philosophically, but rage and indignation took possession of Rashîd. And his indignation was increased by the popularity of our insulter with the girls and teachers of the mission-school hard by. Our guest was innocence itself, if silly and conceited. But Rashîd watched all his movements, and could tell me that the old 'hypocrite,' as he invariably called him, went to the school each day and kissed the pupils, taking the pretty ones upon his knee, and making foolish jokes, talking and giggling like an imbecile, bestowing sweetmeats. With them—for the most sinful motives, as Rashîd averred, and, I suppose, believed—he was all sugar; but when he came back to the house he was as grumpy as could be. Rashîd would have destroyed him at a nod from me one evening when he said:

'I think I must have left my glasses over at the school. Will you be good enough to go and ask?'

'Now your Honour knows how we feel when we meet a man like that; and there are many such among the Franks,' my servant whispered in my ear as I went out obediently. 'By Allah, it is not to be endured!'

The parson occupied the only bedroom; and I slept out upon the balcony on his account. Yet he complained of certain of my garments hanging in his room, and flung them out. It was after that revolting episode, when I was really angry for a moment, that Rashîd came to me and said:

'You hate this hypocrite; is it not so?'

'By Allah,' I replied, 'I hate him.'

He seemed relieved by the decision of my tone, and then informed me:

'I know a person who would kill him for the sake of thirty English pounds.'

It became, of course, incumbent on me to explain that, with us English, hatred is not absolute as with the children of the Arabs—mine had already reached the laughing stage. He was evidently disappointed, and answered with a weary sigh:

'May Allah rid us of this foul oppression!'

It was a bitter pill for him, whose whole endeavour was for my aggrandisement, to see me treated like a menial by our guest; who, one fine evening, had me summoned to his presence—I had been sitting with some village elders in the olive grove behind the house—and made to me a strange proposal, which Rashîd declared by Allah proved his perfect infamy. His manner was for once quite amiable. Leaning back in a deck-chair, his two hands with palms resting on his waistcoat, the fingers raised communicating at the tips, he said, with clerical complacency:

'It is my purpose to make a little tour to visit missionary ladies at three several places in these mountains, and then to go on to Jezzîn to see the waterfall. As you appear to know the country and the people intimately, and can speak the language, it would be well if you came too. The man Rashîd could wait upon us all.'

Rashîd, I knew, was listening at the door.

'Us all? How many of you are there, then?'

He hemmed a moment ere replying:

'I—er—think of taking the Miss Karams with me'—Miss Sara Karam, a young lady of Syrian birth but English education, was head teacher at the girls' school, and her younger sister, Miss Habîbah Karam, was her constant visitor—'I thought you might take charge of the younger of the two. The trip will give them both great pleasure, I am sure.'

And they were going to Jezzîn, where there was no hotel, and we should have to herd together in the village guest-room! What would my Arab friends, censorious in all such matters, think of that?

I told him plainly what I thought of the idea, and what the mountain-folk would think of it and all of us. I told him that I had no wish to ruin any woman's reputation, nor to be forced into unhappy marriage by a public scandal.

He, as a visitor, would go away again; as an old man, and professionally holy, his good name could hardly suffer among English people. But the girls would have to live among the mountaineers, who, knowing of their escapade, would thenceforth scorn them. And as for me——

'But I proposed a mere excursion,' he interpolated. 'I fail to see why you should take this tone about it.'

'Well, I have told you what I think,' was my rejoinder. I then went out and told the story to Rashîd, who heartily applauded my decision, which he had already gathered.

I did not see our simple friend again till after breakfast the next morning. Then he said to me, in something of a contrite tone:

'I have been thinking over what you said last night. I confess I had not thought about the native gossip. I have decided to give up the expedition to Jezzîn. And it has occurred to me that, as you are not going, I could ride your horse. It would save the trouble and expense of hiring one, if you would kindly lend it.'

Taken fairly by surprise, I answered: 'Certainly,' and then went out and told Rashîd what I had done. He wrung his hands and bitterly reproached me.

'But there is one good thing,' he said; 'Sheytân will kill him.'

In all the months that we had owned that horse Rashîd had never once before alluded to him by the name which I had chosen. It was ill-omened, he had often warned me. But nothing could be too ill-omened for that hypocrite.

'I do not want to lend the horse at all,' I said. 'And I am pretty sure he could not ride him. But what was I to say? He took me by surprise.'

'In that case,' said Rashîd, 'all is not said. Our darling shall enjoy his bath today.'

The washing of my horse—a coal-black Arab stallion, as playful as a kitten and as mad—was in the nature of a public festival for all the neighbours. Sheytân was led down to the spring, where all the population gathered, the bravest throwing water over him with kerosene tins, while he plunged and kicked and roused the mountain echoes with his naughty screaming. On this occasion, for a finish, Rashîd let go his hold upon the head-rope, the people fled in all directions, and off went our Sheytân with tail erect, scrambling and careering up the terraces, as nimble as a goat, to take the air before returning to his stable.

Our reverend guest had watched the whole performance from our balcony, which, from a height of some three hundred feet, looked down upon the spring. I was up there behind him, but I said no word till he exclaimed in pious horror:

'What a vicious brute! Dangerous—ought to be shot!' when I inquired to what he was alluding.

'Whose is that savage beast?' he asked, with quite vindictive ire, pointing to Sheytân, who was disporting on the terrace just below.

'Oh, that's my horse,' I answered, interested. 'He's really quite a lamb.'

'Your horse! You don't mean that?'

He said no more just then, but went indoors, and then out to the mission school to see the ladies.

That evening he informed me: 'I shall not require your horse. I had no notion that it was so strong an animal when I suggested borrowing it. Old Câsim at the school will hire one for me. I should be afraid lest such a valuable horse as yours might come to grief while in my charge.'

That was his way of putting it.

We watched the party start one early morning, the clergyman all smiles, the ladies in a flutter, all three mounted on hired chargers of the most dejected type, old Câsim from the school attending them upon a jackass. Rashîd addressed the last-named as he passed our house, applying a disgraceful epithet to his employment. The poor old creature wept.

'God knows,' he said, 'I would not choose such service. But what am I to do? A man must live. And I will save my lady's virtue if I can.'

'May Allah help you!' said Rashîd. 'Take courage; I have robbed his eyes.'

I had no notion of his meaning at the time when, sitting on the balcony, I overheard this dialogue; but later in the day Rashîd revealed to me two pairs of eyeglasses belonging to our guest. Without these glasses, which were of especial power, the reverend man could not see anything in detail.

'And these two pairs were all he had,' exclaimed Rashîd with triumph. 'He always used to put them on when looking amorously at the ladies. The loss of them, please God, will spoil his pleasure.'

The Hanging Dog

Our English host possessed a spaniel bitch, which, being well-bred gave him much anxiety. The fear of *mésalliances* was ever in his mind, and furiously would he drive away the village pariahs when they came slinking round the house, with lolling tongues. One brown and white dog, larger than the others and with bristling hair, was a particular aversion, the thought of which deprived him of his sleep of nights; and not the thought alone, for that persistent suitor—more like a bear than any dog I ever saw—made a great noise around us in the darkness, whining, howling, and even scrabbling at the stable door. At length, in desperation, he resolved to kill him.

One night, when all the village was asleep, we lay out on the balcony with guns and waited. After a while the shadow of a dog slinking among the olive trees was seen. We fired. The village and the mountains echoed; fowls clucked, dogs barked; we even fancied that we heard the cries of men. We expected the whole commune to rise up against us; but after a short time of waiting all was still again.

Rashîd, out in the shadows, whispered: 'He is nice and fat,' as if he thought that we were going to eat the dog.

'And is he dead?' I asked.

'Completely dead,' was the reply.

'Then get a cord and hang him to the balcony,' said my companion. 'His odour will perhaps attract the foxes.'

Another minute and the corpse was hanging from the balcony, while we lay out and waited, talking in low tones.

The bark of foxes came from vineyards near at hand, where there were unripe grapes. 'Our vines have tender grapes,' our host repeated; making me think of the fable of the fox and the grapes, which I related to Rashîd in Arabic as best I could. He laughed as he exclaimed:

'Ripe grapes, you say? Our foxes do not love ripe grapes and seldom steal them. I assure you, it was sour grapes that the villain wanted, and never did they seem so exquisitely sour as when he found out that he could not reach them. How his poor mouth watered!'

This was new light upon an ancient theme for us, his hearers.

After an hour or two of idle waiting, when no foxes came, we went to bed, forgetting all about the hanging dog.

The house was close beside a carriage road which leads down from the chief town of the mountains to the city, passing many villages. As it was summer, when the wealthy citizens sleep in the mountain villages for coolness' sake, from the dawn onward there was a downward stream of carriages along that road. When the daylight became strong enough for men to see distinctly, the sight of a great brown and white dog hanging from our balcony, and slowly turning, struck terror in the breasts of passers-by. Was it a sign of war, or some enchantment? Carriage after carriage stopped, while its inhabitants attempted to explore the mystery. But there was nobody about to answer questions. My host and I, Rashîd as well, were fast asleep indoors. Inquirers looked around them on the ground, and then up at the shuttered house and then at the surrounding olive trees, in one of which they finally espied a nest of bedding on which reclined a blue-robed man asleep. It was the cook, Amîn, who slept there for fresh air. The firing of the night before had not disturbed him.

By dint of throwing stones they woke him up, and he descended from his tree and stood before them, knuckling his eyes, which were still full of sleep.

They asked: 'What means this portent of the hanging dog?'

He stared incredulously at the object of their wonder, then exclaimed: 'Some enemy has done it, to insult me, while I slept. No matter, I will be avenged before the day is out.'

The tidings of the mystery ran through the village, and every able-bodied person came to view it, and express opinions.

'The dog is well known. He is called Barûd; he was the finest in our village. He used to guard the dwelling of *Sheykh* Ali till he transferred his pleasure to the house of *Sheykh* Selîm. It was a sin to kill him,' was the general verdict. And Amîn confirmed it, saying: 'Aye, a filthy sin. But I will be avenged before the day is out.'

At last Rashîd, awakened by the noise of talking, came out of the stable where he always slept, and with a laugh explained the whole occurrence. Some of the villagers were greatly shocked, and blamed us strongly. But Rashîd stood up for us, declaring that the dog belonged in truth to no man, so that no man living had the right to blame his murderer; whereas the valuable sporting bitch of the *Casîs* (our host) was all his own, and it was his duty therefore to defend her from improper lovers. He then cut down the body of the dog, which no one up till then had dared to do; and all the people gradually went away.

The coast was clear when we arose towards eight o'clock. Rashîd, with laughter, told the tale to us at breakfast. We had been silly, we agreed, to leave the hanging dog; and there, as we supposed, the matter ended.

But hardly had we finished breakfast when a knock came at the open door, and we beheld a tall and dignified *fellâh* depositing his staff against the doorpost and shuffling off his slippers at the call to enter.

He said the murdered dog was his, and dear to him as his own eyes, his wife and children. He was the finest dog in all the village, of so rare a breed that no one in the world had seen a dog just like him. He had been of use to guard the house, and for all kinds of work. The *fellâh* declared his worth to be five Turkish pounds, which we must pay immediately unless we wished our crime to be reported to the Government.

With as nonchalant an air as I could muster, I offered him a *beshlik*—fourpence halfpenny. He thereupon became abusive and withdrew—in the end, hurriedly, because Rashîd approached him in a hostile manner.

He had not been gone ten minutes when another peasant came, asserting that the dog was really his, and he had been on the point of regaining his possession by arbitration of the neighbours when we shot the animal. He thus considered himself doubly injured—in his expectations and his property. He came to ask us instantly to pay an English pound, or he would lay the case before the Turkish governor, with whom, he could assure us, he had favour.

I offered him the *beshlik*, and he also stalked off in a rage.

We were still discussing these encounters with Rashîd when there arrived a vastly more imposing personage—no other than the headman of the village, the correct *Sheykh* Mustafa, who had heard, he said, of the infamous attempts which had been made to levy blackmail on us, and came now in all haste to tell us of the indignation and disgust which such dishonesty towards foreigners aroused in him. He could assure us that the dog was really his; and he was glad that we had shot the creature, since to shoot it gave us pleasure. His one desire was that we should enjoy ourselves. Since our delight was in the slaughter of domestic animals, he proposed to bring his mare—of the best blood of the desert—round for us to shoot.

We felt exceedingly ashamed, and muttered what we could by way of an apology. But the *sheykh* would not accept it from us. Gravely smiling, and stroking his grey beard, he said: 'Nay, do what pleases you. God knows, your pleasure is a law to us. Nay, speak the word, and almost (God forgive me!) I would bring my little son for you to shoot. So unlimited is my regard for men so much above the common rules of this our county, and who are protected in their every fancy by the Powers of Europe.'

His flattery dejected us for many days.

84

TIGERS

The *fellâhîn* who came to gossip in the winter evenings round our lamp and stove assured us there were tigers in the neighbouring mountain. We, of course, did not accept the statement literally, but our English friend possessed the killing instinct, and held that any feline creatures which could masquerade in popular report as tigers would afford him better sport than he had yet enjoyed in Syria. So when the settled weather came we went to look for them.

For my part I take pleasure in long expeditions with a gun, though nothing in the way of slaughter come of them. My lack of keenness at the proper moment has been the scorn and the despair of native guides and hunters. Once, in Egypt, at the inundation of the Nile, I had been rowed for miles by eager men, and had lain out an hour upon an islet among reeds, only to forget to fire when my adherents whispered as the duck flew over, because the sun was rising and the desert hills were blushing like the rose against a starry sky. I had chased a solitary partridge a whole day among the rocks of En-gedi without the slightest prospect of success; and in the Jordan valley I had endured great hardships in pursuit of wild boar without seeing one. It was the lurking in wild places at unusual hours which pleased me, not the matching of my strength and skill against the might of beasts. I have always been averse to every sort of competition. This I explain that all may know that, though I sallied forth with glee in search of savage creatures, it was not to kill them.

We set out from our village on a fine spring morning,

attended by Rashîd, my servant, and a famous hunter of the district named Muhammad, also two mules, which carried all things necessary for our camping out, and were in charge of my friend's cook, Amîn by name. We rode into the mountains, making for the central range of barren heights, which had the hue and something of the contour of a lion's back. At length we reached a village at the foot of this commanding range, and asked for tigers. We were told that they were farther on. A man came with us to a point of vantage whence he was able to point out the very place—a crag in the far distance floating in a haze of heat. After riding for a day and a half we came right under it, and at a village near its base renewed inquiry. 'Oh,' we were told, 'the tigers are much farther on. You see that eminence?' Again a mountain afar off was indicated. At the next village we encamped, for night drew near. The people came out to inspect us, and we asked them for the tigers.

'Alas!' they cried. 'It is not here that you must seek them. By Allah, you are going in the wrong direction. Behold that distant peak!'

And they pointed to the place from which we had originally started.

Our English friend was much annoyed, Rashîd and the *shikâri* and the cook laughed heartily. No one, however, was for going back. Upon the following day our friend destroyed a jackal and two conies, which consoled him somewhat in the dearth of tigers, and we rode forward resolutely, asking our question at each village as we went along. Everywhere we were assured that there were really tigers in the mountain, and from some of the villages young sportsmen who owned guns insisted upon joining our excursion, which showed that they themselves believed such game existed. But their adherence, though it gave us hope, was tiresome, for they smoked our cigarettes and ate our food.

At last, towards sunset on the seventh evening of our expedition, we saw a wretched-looking village on the heights with no trees near it, and only meagre strips of cultivation on little terraces, like ledges, of the slope below.

Our friend had just been telling me that he was weary of this wild-goose chase, with all the rascals upon earth adhering to us. He did not now believe that there were tigers in the mountain, nor did I. And we had quite agreed to start for home upon the morrow, when the people of that miserable village galloped down to greet us with delighted shouts, as if they had been waiting for us all their lives.

'What is your will?' inquired the elders of the place, obsequiously.

'Tigers,' was our reply. 'Say, O old man, are there any tigers in your neighbourhood?'

The old man flung up both his hands to heaven, and his face became transfigured as in ecstasy. He shouted: 'Is it tigers you desire? This, then, is the place where you will dwell content. Tigers? I should think so! Tigers everywhere!'

The elders pointed confidently to the heights, and men and women—even children—told us: 'Aye, by Allah! Hundreds—thousands of them; not just one or two. As many as the most capacious man could possibly devour in forty years.'

'It looks as if we'd happened right at last,' our friend said, smiling for the first time in three days.

We pitched our tent upon the village threshing-floor, the only flat place, except roofs of houses, within sight. The village elders dined with us, and stayed till nearly midnight, telling us about the tigers and the way to catch them. Some of the stories they related were incredible, but not much more so than is usual in that kind of narrative. It seemed unnecessary for one old man to warn us gravely on no account to take them by their tails.

'For snakes it is the proper way,' he said sagaciously, 'since snakes can only double half their length. But tigers double their whole length, and they object to it. To every creature its own proper treatment.'

But there was no doubt of the sincerity of our instructors, nor of their eagerness to be of use to us in any way. Next morning, when we started out, the headman came with us some distance, on purpose to instruct the guide he had assigned to us, a stupid-looking youth, who seemed afraid. He told him: 'Try first over there among the boulders, and when you have exhausted that resort, go down to the ravine, and thence beat upwards to the mountain-top. Please God, your Honours will return with half a hundred of those tigers which devour our crops.'

Thus sped with hope, we set out in good spirits, expecting not a bag of fifty tigers, to speak truly, but the final settlement of a dispute which had long raged among us, as to what those famous tigers really were. Rashîd would have it they were leopards, I said lynxes, and our English friend, in moments of depression, thought of polecats. But, though we scoured the mountain all that day, advancing with the utmost caution and in open order, as our guide enjoined, we saw no creature of the feline tribe. Lizards, basking motionless upon the rocks, slid off like lightning when aware of our approach. Two splendid eagles from an eyrie on the crags above hovered and wheeled, observing us, their shadows like two moving spots of ink upon the mountain-side. A drowsy owl was put up from a cave, and one of our adherents swore he heard a partridge calling. No other living creature larger than a beetle did we come across that day.

Returning to the camp at evening, out of temper, we were met by all the village, headed by the *sheykh*, who loudly hoped that we had had good sport, and brought home many tigers to provide a feast. When he heard that we had not so much as seen a single one he fell upon the luckless youth who had been told off to conduct us, and would have slain him, I believe, had we not intervened.

'Didst seek in all the haunts whereof I told you ? Well I know you did not, since they saw no tiger! Behold our faces blackened through your sloth and folly, O abandoned beast!'

Restrained by force by two of our adherents, the *sheykh* spat venomously at the weeping guide, who swore by Allah that he had obeyed instructions to the letter.

Our English friend was much too angry to talk Arabic. He bade me tell the *sheykh* he was a liar, and that the country was as bare of tigers as his soul of truth. Some of our *fellâh* adherents seconded my speech. The *sheykh* appeared amazed and greatly horrified.

'There are tigers,' he assured us, 'naturally! All that you desire.'

'Then go and find them for us!' said our friend, vindictively.

'Upon my head,' replied the complaisant old man, laying his right hand on his turban reverently. 'To hear is to obey.'

We regarded this reply as mere politeness, the affair as ended. What was our surprise next morning to see the *sheykh* and all the able men, accompanied by many children, set off up the mountain armed with staves and scimitars, and all the antique armament the village boasted! It had been our purpose to depart that day, but we remained to watch the outcome of that wondrous hunting.

The villagers spread out and 'beat' the mountain. All day long we heard their shouts far off among the upper heights. If any tiger had been there they must assuredly have roused him. But they returned at evening empty-handed, and as truly crestfallen as if they had indeed expected to bring home a bag of fifty tigers. One man presented me with a dead owl—the same, I think, which we had startled on the day before, as if to show that their display had not been quite in vain.

'No tigers!' sighed the *sheykh*, as though his heart were broken. 'What can have caused them all to go away? Unhappy day!' A lamentable wail went up from the whole crowd. 'A grievous disappointment, but the world is thus. But,' he added, with a sudden brightening, 'if your Honours will but condescend to stay a week or two, no doubt they will return.'

PRIDE AND A FALL

There was to be a grand fantasia at the castle of the greatest of *Druze sheykhs* in honour of a visit from the English Consul-General in Syria; and as an Englishman I was invited to be there. It was a journey of a day and a half. Upon the second morning Rashîd and I had not gone far ere we fell in with other horsemen wending in the same direction as ourselves, well mounted and in holiday attire. All greeted us politely, but we kept apart, because they nearly all rode mares while we rode stallions—a fruitful source of trouble and a cause of war.

At length a young man mounted on a stallion overtook us with most cordial greetings. I had met him often. He was the son of a rich landowner in a neighbouring valley, and, I think, the most beautiful human creature I ever saw. That day he was particularly good to look at, his complexion of clear olive slightly flushed, his violet eyes beneath their long dark lashes dancing, his perfect white teeth gleaming with excitement and delight. He wore a cloak, broad striped, of white and crimson, a white frilled shirt of lawn showing above a vest of crimson velvet, fawn-coloured baggy trousers, and soft sheepskin boots. A snow-white turban crowned his whole appearance. His horse was thoroughbred and young, and he controlled its ceaseless dance to admiration. He told me that the stallion was his own, an uncle's gift, and quite the best in all the mountains; although mine, he added out of mere politeness, was undoubtedly a pearl of breeding and high spirit. He hoped with such a steed to gain renown in that day's horsemanship, and, if it might be, win the notice of the Consul-General and his lady.

'My father wished me to take out another horse,' he said; 'but I love this one, and am used to all his ways. I could not do myself full justice on another, nor would Rustem do his best for any other rider.'

He proceeded to discuss the horses which we saw before us on the road, pointing out in each of them some defect, and exclaiming: 'I shall excel them all, *in sh'Allah!* Does not your Honour also think my horse the best?'

I assured him that I did indeed, and all my wishes were for his success, 'because,' said I, 'I know and like you, and I do not know the others.'

'But some you know for a certainty, for all the Mountain will be there. Come, let me name them to you one by one.' And some of those he named were certainly well known to me.

'When you see Hasan, son of Ali, nicely mounted, will you not think he is the better man?'

'No, no, by Allah!' I disclaimed such fickleness. 'Be sure that if good wishes can ensure success, all mine are with you in today's event.'

'Allah increase your wealth!' he cried in joy, as if I had bestowed on him a gift of price.

There was a crowd of many colours on the well-made road which wanders up through orchards to the village and ends on the *meydân* before the castle gate. There the crowd halted, making fast their horses to the many rings and tie-holes which were in the walls. Rashîd took charge of my horse and his own, while I went on up steps on to a higher platform intersected by a stream of ice-cold water plunging down into the valley in a fine cascade whose spray and murmur cooled the air. That rush of water was the greatest luxury in such a land, and the lord of the castle took much pride in its contrivance.

I went up to a door where soldiers and domestics lounged, but was informed: 'Our lord is out of doors.' A soldier pointed to a bunch of trees above the waterfall and overlooking the *meydân*, where many notables in black frock coat and *fez* sat out on chairs. He ran on to announce my coming. I was soon a member of the formal group, replying to the usual compliments and kind inquiries.

Coffee was handed round. Then came a tray of different kinds of sherbet, then a tray of eatables. The chiefs around me talked of harvests and the price of land, but, most of all, of horses, since it was a horsey day. The screaming of a stallion came persistently from the *meydân*—a naughty screaming which foreboded mischief. I recognised the voice. The culprit was my own Sheytân. The screams were so disturbing, so indecent, that several of the great ones round me frowned and asked: 'Whose horse is that?' in accents of displeasure. I was ashamed to own him.

At length the lord of the castle called a servant to his side and whispered, pointing with his hand in the direction whence the screams proceeded. The servant hurried off, but presently returned and whispered something in his master's ear. His master looked at me and nodded gravely. He then addressed me in a deprecating tone, remarking: 'Your Honour's horse is too high-spirited; the crowd excites him. Will you allow him to be tethered in some other place?'

From the excessive smoothness of his manner I could guess that, had I been a native of the land, he would have told me to remove the vicious brute and myself likewise. I rose at once to go and see to it.

'Pray do not give yourself the trouble!' he exclaimed, distressed.

The servant went along with me, and, when we got to the *meydân*, Rashîd came running. Sheytân was then indeed a terrifying sight, with streaming tail, mane bristling, and a wicked bloodshot eye, tearing at his head-rope, one minute pawing at the wall as if to climb it, the next kicking wildly with his head down. I know little of horses in general, but I knew that particular horse, and he knew me. I went up quietly and talked to him, then loosed the rope and led Sheytân away without much difficulty, Rashîd meanwhile explaining to the servant of the house that no one else could possibly have done it. We tied him at the further end of the *meydân*.

Then I went back on to the terrace, where the notables had risen and were looking at the youths who were to take part in the fantasia, among them my companion of the road, the young *Sheykh* Abdul Hamid. These were now on the parade-ground with their horses. My neighbour in the group of great ones said, politely:

'Your Honour should go with them; it is only proper, since their going is to compliment the representative of England. And you are, I see, a very skilful cavalier. The way you quieted that horse of yours was wonderful. We have all been talking of it. Ride with them!'

I begged to be excused. The essence of the fantasia is to show off one's own prowess and one's horse's paces while careering madly in a widish circle round some given object—an open carriage with some great one in it, or a bridal pair—taking no note of obstacles, dashing over rocks and gullies and down breakneck slopes, loading and firing off a gun at intervals, in full career. I had tried the feeling of it once at a friend's wedding, and had been far from happy, though my horse enjoyed the romp and often tried to start it afterwards when there was no occasion. Remembering Abdul Hamid and his desire for praise that day, I said:

'There is only one good horseman here—Abdul Hamid, the son of the *Sheykh* Mustafa. All the rest of us, compared with him, are mere pedestrians.'

I pointed out the youth in question to my neighbour, who was a man of power in the mountains, and he praised the beauty of his form on horseback.

'By Allah, right is with you,' he assented. 'There is none but he.'

Away they went—*Jinblâts, Talhûks*, and *Abdul Meliks*—all in clean white turbans, with coloured cloaks a-stream upon the breeze, on horses gorgeously caparisoned. We waited half an hour—in silence, as it seemed; and then we heard the noise of their return, the shouts, the firing. I swear I saw a horse and man surmount a housetop in the village and then leap down upon the other side. At last, with yells and reckless gunshots and a whirl of dust, the crowd of horsemen came full tilt on the *meydân*. Their leader—in appearance a mad angel—was my friend, Abdul Hamid. Suddenly he drew his rein, flinging the steed right back upon his haunches. In so doing, looking up at me with a triumphant smile, he somehow missed his balance and pitched clear over his horse's head, just at the very moment when a carriage and pair containing the beaming Consul-General and his lady, with a glorious *Cawwâs* upon the box, arrived upon the scene. I ran to help him, but another person was before me. A tall old man, whose garb bespoke him an initiated *Druze*, rushed out among the horses and the dust and beat the wretched lad about the shoulders, heaping curses on that lovely head for bringing shame upon an honoured house before such company. It was the lad's own father, the *Sheykh* Mustafa. I helped to drag the old man off, and would have gone on to console the son; but just then I beheld Sheytân approaching with a broken head-rope. I contrived to catch him and to mount without attending to the girths; and, once on horseback, I was glad to be there; for quite fifty of the tethered steeds had broken loose in the excitement, and were rushing here and there and fighting in a most alarming way. I have always had a dread of horse-fights, and this was not a single fight; it was a mêlée, fresh horses every minute breaking loose to join it. Right in my way two angry stallions rose up, boxing one another like the lion and the unicorn, and a little boy of ten or thereabouts ran in between and, jumping, caught their head-ropes.

I escaped at last and rode down through the village to the bottom of the valley, where a grove of walnut trees cast pleasant shade beside a stream. There Rashîd found me later in the day. He told me that my disappearance had caused consternation and alarm, the Consul-General and his lady having asked for me. Bidding him remain with the two horses, I went back on foot to the castle, where I stayed only the time necessary to pay my respects.

As I was returning towards the valley, a litter borne between two mules was leaving the *meydân*. Beside it walked the stern *Sheykh* Mustafa, and in it, I had little doubt, reclined the beautiful Abdul Hamid.

I asked the serving-man who led the foremost mule if his young lord was seriously hurt. He answered:

'Yes; for he has broken his elbow and his shoulder and his collar-bone. But that is nothing, since he has disgraced our house.'

A bitter wail of 'Woe the day!' came from within the palanquin.

TRAGEDY

The sun was sinking down over the sea, the mountain wall with all its clefts and promontories wore a cloak of many colours, when we saw before us on a rock a ruined tower. We were looking for some human habitation where we might get food and shelter for the night; but we should have passed by that building, taking it to be deserted, had not we espied a woman's figure sitting out before it in the evening light.

Experience of late had taught us to shun villages, belonging thereabouts to a peculiar sect, whose members made a virtue of inhospitality. At noon that day, when wishing to buy food, we had been met with such amazing insults that Rashîd, my henchman, had not yet recovered from his indignation, and still brooded on revenge. On seeing that the ruined tower had occupants, he said:

'If these refuse us, we will force an entrance mercilessly; for see, they dwell alone, with none to help them.'

He rode before me towards the tower, with shoulders squared and whip upraised.

It surprised me that the woman sitting out before the door appeared indifferent to his approach, until, upon a closer view, I saw that she was old and blind. She must, I thought, be deaf as well, since she had failed to move at sound of hoof beats; which sound brought out an aged man, who shattered Rashîd's plan of vengeance by exclaiming: *Itfaddalû!* (Perform a kindness!' that is, 'Enter!').

'It is you who does kindness,' I replied, by rote. 'We are your suppliants for food and rest this night.'

'All mine is thine,' the old man answered, coming to hold my horse's head, while I dismounted. His wrinkled face was moulded to a patient, sad expression, which became more noticeable when he smiled; and he was always smiling.

I went into the tower and down a flight of much-worn steps, which ended in a heap of fallen masonry.

'Deign to proceed,' called out the tenant from behind me; when, climbing over the obstruction, I found myself in a large room, of which the only furniture consisted in a heap of bedding and some cooking things. Rather to my surprise the place was clean. The old man flung himself upon the ground and blew upon the mass of charcoal in a brazier, and presently a smell of coffee stewing filled the dungeon; for such it doubtless had been in the past, its only window being high above our heads, yet only just above the level of the rock, as I discovered when I went to seek Rashîd, who, by our host's direction, had bestowed the horses in a cavern by the sea. The blind old woman still sat out before the door.

I walked all round the tower and noticed small fields neatly fenced below it on the landward side, and a few hobbled goats upon a strip of herbage near the shore; which, with some fishing-nets spread out upon the rocks to dry, informed me how our host obtained a livelihood.

As I went back towards the door, I met Rashîd bringing our saddlebags. He nodded to the woman, who still sat there motionless, and told me: 'She is mad, the poor old creature—but not dangerous. Fear nothing. They are quite good people. It is strange, but he informs me she is not his mother nor his wife, nor anyone by birth allied to him. And yet he waits upon her, helpless as she is.'

Just then, the master of the tower appeared, and, going to the woman, took her hand and raised her. '*Itfaddalû!*' he said, with just the same polite alacrity with which he welcomed us on our arrival, as if she, too, had been an honoured guest. We all went down the broken steps into the dungeon. A meal of fish and bread was set before us. The woman took her food apart. The master of the house did not sit down till she was satisfied; and, after supper, he set out a bed for her, and then washed out the vessels, before he came again and sat with us. By that time the old woman was asleep. Two lighted wicks, passed through a piece of cork which floated in a bowl of oil and water, roused the shadows of the vault. A sudden outcry at the far end of the room made us both jump.

'Fear nothing!' said our entertainer. 'She is dreaming. Ah, poor lady! Our Lord repay her goodness in the next life for all the evil she has borne in this!'

'Is it permissible to ask to hear her story?' said Rashîd.

The old man looked at me with a reluctant smile, as who should say: 'It is a sad tale. Would you really care to hear it?'

I nodded gravely, and, with a deep sigh, he began:

'Many years ago—how many it is now impossible for me to say, for, dwelling here, I have lost count of time—a certain chieftain of the desert Arabs had a son who loved the daughter of his father's enemy. There was no intercourse between the houses, but the young prince of whom I speak contrived to see the maiden and to meet her stealthily, even riding in among the dwellings of her people at risk of his own life and mine; for I must tell you that I am his foster-brother, though not by blood a scion of the desert, and so I served him, as was usual with us, in the quality of an esquire.

'Both tribes were of those Arabs which have villages for their headquarters, without renouncing the old life of war and wandering. Our village was upon the borders of the Belka, and hers far north towards the Hauran. In those days there were no Turkish military posts beyond the Jordan. The feuds and customs of the tribes were then the only law; though now, they tell me, that that country is made safe for travel.

'There was no means to bridge the gulf which custom fixed between the lovers; and so my foster-brother, being mad with longing for the maid, decided to abduct her and escape into the settled country. I, loving him, applauded all his schemes. The princess Amîneh—for she was the daughter of a sovereign chief—was of a spirit equal to his own. She rode out from her father's town by night upon the best mare of the tribe with but one girl attendant. My lord and I were waiting by a certain well. And then we rode, well knowing that both tribes would hunt us, towards the *wilâyet*, where there was law and Turkish power to protect us. The princess Amîneh lacked a man's endurance, and her woman suffered greatly from fatigue. Their weakness had to be considered, and there came a time when it was evident that they could go no further without rest.

'We were then within a short day's journey of the nearest Government post, attaining which we should have been in safety. We took refuge in a ruined sheepcote. I was keeping the look-out while all the others slept, when I noticed a small cloud of dust uprising in the distance. I roused my lord, and told him: "The pursuers come." He looked upon the princess and her maiden: they lay fast asleep, exhausted by fatigue.

'"Let be," he said. "There is no hope for us in flight. Lie low. Perhaps they will pass by without perceiving us."

'And so they might have done, God knows, had not our horses neighed, winding the other horses.'

The old man wrung his hands, then hid his eyes with them.

'Never, never can I tell the details of what followed. We fought, and the princess fought beside us, snatching a scimitar which I was wearing from my side. Her boldness helped us somewhat to delay the end, for our assailants were her father's people, and they feared to hurt her. But the end came; it was from the first inevitable. I was lying helpless on the ground, wounded, but fully conscious, when they slew my lord. At once they hewed his body into fragments, each of which was soon exalted on a spear. The princess, wounded in the face, and pinioned, witnessed that. Her damsel lay inanimate, and at the time I thought her dead. She was my promised bride. Then the Emir approached with a great spear—as I suppose, to kill his daughter, but just then there were loud shouts, and then another battle, in which I heard the war-cry of our tribe. The father of my lord, pursuing also with intent to punish us, had come upon his ancient enemy at unawares. He won the day. The other Arabs broke and fled. The noblest of our braves pursued them; but several of the lewder sort remained behind to torture and dishonour my unhappy lady. I tried to rise and rescue her, but, with the effort, my spirit left my body, and I lay as dead—the praise to Allah!—which is the reason why I am alive today.

'So great a fight could not take place so near the guarded country without coming to the knowledge of the Government. Ten Turkish soldiers, armed with carbines, and an *ombashi*, coming to the spot next day, discovered us, and carried the survivors to a place of safety. The princess was then, as you yourselves have seen her, except that she was young and now is old. Her damsel had survived the fight without much hurt, by God's protection, having lain upon the ground so still that she was left for dead. When I recovered from my wounds, I married her.

'So tragic was our tale that all men pitied us. The

Governor himself protected the princess, and placed her with the women of his household. But she could not be happy in the city, in that kind of life; her soul grew restless, pining. My wife, who visited her every day, was grieved for her; and when I found that it was as she said, I went and asked the Governor's permission to support our lady. Perceiving that she was not happy in his house, he yielded; and we three wandered through the settled country for long months, the people showing kindness to us through compassion, for our tale was known. At last we reached this ruin by the sea, which pleased our lady because, my wife believed, the mountains are so like a wall raised up between her and the country of her grief. That must be thirty years ago; but she has never wandered since.

'My wife died and I buried her beside the shore; for years I have performed her duties to our lady. The people of these parts are wicked, but they let us be, because they think that we are under some enchantment. My prayer is always that I may survive my lady, for how could she, poor creature, fare alone? So far, we have been very fortunate, praise be to Allah!'

Rashîd was loud in his expressions of amazement at the story, his mind intent upon the central tragedy. He said no word of praise or wonder at our host's self-sacrifice. That he accepted, as a thing of course. This attitude of his, which I observed, prevented me from uttering the words of pity and condolence which were on my tongue; and I am glad those words were never uttered, for they were impertinent, and would have seemed absurd to Orientals, who have not our sentiment.

So, after the conclusion of the tale, we went to bed.

BASTIRMA

The moon began to shine upon the gardens of Damascus, casting pale shadows, though the daylight had not quite departed, and the sky behind the trees to westward was still green. We were sitting out on stools under the walnut trees, beside a stream which made a pleasant murmur. The air was laden with the scent of unseen roses. Behind us was a little tavern with a lantern lighted in its entrance arch, a solitary yellow eye amid the twilight.

We were the centre of a crowd, as usual when Suleymân was with us. His voice attracted people like a drum, and the matter of his talk had power to hold them. It was a weighty voice of studied modulations, which promised wisdom on the brink of laughter. He generally chose some moral or religious subject for discourse, and illustrated it by what we call 'nawâdir' selected from his vast experience of life. By his own account he had journeyed to the world's rim, and had associated not alone with men, but also with *jinn* and ghouls. On the other hand, he had been to Europe several times, and knew the streets of Paris and of London. Somehow, one never doubted any of his stories while he was telling them, the accents of his voice had such conviction. One was conscious that his tales—even the most extravagant—were true in some mysterious, intrinsic way. This time he chose to speak to us of guilt and innocence, of good and evil works, and their effect on man's salvation. He aired the theory, which roused approving murmurs in the listening circle, that to have a good intention was the chief desideratum for every son of

Adam on his journey through the world, no matter though his works might turn out bad or unsuccessful.

'To lie with good intention is better than to tell the truth with bad intention,' he declared.

'To lie is the salt of a man; the shame is to him who believes,' put in Rashîd, my servant, who was great at proverbs.

Suleymân paid no heed to the interruption.

'A sin committed thoughtlessly,' said he, 'is light compared with one which you have hatched and planned.'

'Nay, O beloved, a sin is a sin, appointed so by the Most High; and the duty of a man is to avoid it. The hurt to man's salvation is the same, however he approach it,' said an old man in the audience. 'If I cut my hand, is the wound less, is it not rather likely to be more—for being thoughtless?'

There was a murmur of applause as all eyes turned on this objector, whose likeness could not be distinguished in the gloaming.

I spoke in approbation of the view expressed, and the old man, emboldened, laughed:

'To lie is bad, to kill is bad, to steal is bad. Our Lord destroy this rogue of an Intention, which plain men cannot catch nor understand!'

'Nay, listen!' Suleymân became persuasive and profoundly earnest, as was his manner always under opposition. 'You have not altogether caught my meaning. I say a man should trust in the Most High, not think too much beforehand of his ways. By thinking beforehand, he may form a bad intention, since man's thoughts are naturally fallible. Let him think afterwards, thus he will learn to shun such snares in future, and by repentance place a good work to his credit. Men learn wisdom from their sins, not from their righteous deeds. And the consciousness of sin, the knowledge that they may at any moment fall into it, preserves them from the arrogance of goodness.'

'There may be some small grain of sense in what you say,' chuckled the objector, 'but not enough to make sin righteous, nor yet to abrogate the sacred law.'

Suleymân pursued unheeding: 'I have a rare thing, which will show you what I mean.

'A new judge had been appointed to the Holy City. He was departing from Stambûl by ship to take up his appointment. On the quay, a Jew of his acquaintance came to him with reverence, and begged him kindly to convey a basket of *bastirma* to his (the Jew's) son at the Holy City, which the Jews in their own language call Jerusalem. You all know what *bastirma* is. It is dried and salted mutton—very tasty—a dish of which the Turks are most inordinately fond. The *Cadi* graciously consented, bidding his major-domo take the basket, and bestow it carefully among the things. The Jew departed. The *Cadi* and his party journeyed till they reached their destination, where, upon arrival, they discovered a young Jew inquiring earnestly about a basket of *bastirma*. The *Cadi* had forgotten its existence. "Ah, to be sure!" he cried. "I gave it my major-domo for safe keeping."

'He called that servant, and commanded him to give the basket of *bastirma* to the Jew there waiting. The major-domo bowed his head, folded his hands upon his breast, and said: "I ask forgiveness, O my lord. The basket still remains, but the *bastirma* was so excellent that, having tasted but a piece of it, I wanted more, so that, in fact, I ate it all upon the journey. I wish to pay the price of it to this young Jew."

'The *Cadi* thought his servant's offer fair enough, but the young Jew went mad. Flying at the throat of the major-domo, he flung him to the ground, and tried to tear the soul out of his body with his teeth and nails. The *Cadi* called upon the bystanders for help. The Jew was dragged with difficulty from his victim. Then the *Cadi* asked:

"'Why, pray, did you attack my servant in that savage way?"

"'That man," said the Jew, still white with rage, and pointing with his tallow finger at the major-domo, who had risen from the ground—"that man contains my grandfather."

"'What words are these? Explain yourself!" the *Cadi* cried.

"'Three weeks ago, O gracious Excellency, my grandfather died in Stambûl. It had ever been his dearest wish to be buried in the Holy City, near the scene of judgment; and that wish of his was law on us his offspring. But how could we fulfil it? How, I ask? No skipper, whether Nazarene or Muslim, would receive a dead Jew on his ship for less than the corpse-weight in gold. And we are poor. To take him overland was quite impossible. And so my father and my mother in Stambûl cured his dead limbs, and made of them *bastirma*, and sent him hither in the way you know. It follows that your servant has committed a most dreadful crime. Let him be killed, I pray, and buried in the tomb we have prepared, that so my grandfather's great wish may be fulfilled."

'The major-domo was more dead than living as he heard that story. He rent his clothes and fell down on the ground insensible.

'The *Cadi* answered the young Jew with wisdom, saying: " you are entitled to the price of one basket of *bastirma*, and no more, from this my servant; but he, on his side, has a right to all you own. What wealth can ever compensate him for the haunting fear that on the Last Day he may rise inextricably mingled with your worthy grandfather? Go, I say, and never venture to approach him anymore, or I shall surely act upon this judgment and denude you quite." The major-domo—'

Cries of '*Miskîn! Miskîn!*' (poor fellow!) interrupted the narrative.

One said: 'I once ate pig's flesh by mistake, but this man's plight is much more horrible.'

Suleymân's opponent cried: 'It was a judgment on him, evidently, for his theft of the *bastirma*. Say, what became of him thereafter, O narrator?'

'The major-domo, who, till then, had been a precious rogue—I knew him intimately from a child, and so can vouch for it—became from that day forth the saintliest of men. He thought about his crime and mourned for it, and deemed himself an unclean beast until he died—may God have mercy on him—and was buried in the Holy City as the Jew desired. He thought of nothing but good deeds, yet without seeking merit, knowing that nothing he could do would ever cleanse him. He became the humblest and the best of men, who had before been arrogant and very wicked. Therefore I say that it is well for men to think of their sins after rather than before committing them.'

'But the intention!—What of the intention, O my master? His intention was not good. He stole!'

'His intention went no further than a basket of *bastirma*. The Jew was only an unpleasant accident, in respect whereof no guilt attached to him. The case is clear, and yet, although I used to argue with him on the subject, I never could contrive to make him see it. One thing is certain, and will prove to you the worth of good intentions. He only meant to eat a basket of *bastirma*; therefore he felt great remorse when he devoured a Jew, and so became a saint for Paradise. Had he intended to devour a Jew he could not possibly have felt such great remorse. What say you?'

And everyone agreed that it was so.

THE ARTIST-DRAGOMAN

Of Suleymân in his capacity of dragoman I saw little but heard much both from himself and others. The English residents in Palestine and Syria—those who knew of him—regarded him as but a doubtful character, if one may judge from their repeated warnings to me not to trust him out of sight. His wisdom and his independent way of airing it did not please everybody as they did me; and reverence in dealing with a fellow-man was not his strong point. By travellers, I gather from innumerable testimonials which he showed me, he was either much beloved or the reverse, though none could say he did not know his business.

His English, though voluminous and comprehensive, was sometimes strange to native English ears. He had read the Bible in a German mission school, and spoke of 'Billiam's donkey' and 'the mighty Simson' where we should speak of Balaam's ass and Samson. He called the goatskins used for carrying water 'beastly skins,' and sometimes strengthened a mild sentence with an expletive.

I do not think he ever went so far in this way as another dragoman who, riding out from Haifa one fine morning with an English lady, pointed to Mount Carmel and observed:

'Bloody fine hill, madam!'

He knew how to adapt his language to his audience. But it is curious that a man whose speech in Arabic was highly mannered, in English should have cultivated solecisms.

That he did cultivate them as an asset of his stock-in-trade I can affirm, for he would invent absurd mistakes and then rehearse them to me, with the question: 'Is that funny? Will that make the English laugh?'

For clergymen he kept a special manner and a special store of jokes. When leading such through Palestine he always had a Bible up before him on the saddle; and every night would join them after dinner and preach a sermon on the subject of the next day's journey. This he would make as comical as possible for their amusement, for clergymen, he often used to say to me, are fond of laughter of a certain kind.

One English parson he bedevilled utterly by telling him the truth—or the accepted legend—in such a form that it seemed false or mad to him.

As they were riding out from Jaffa towards Jerusalem, he pointed to the mud-built village of Latrûn and said:

'That, sir, is the place where Simpson catch the foxes.'

'Ah?' said the clergyman. 'And who was Simpson?'

'He was a very clever gentleman, and liked a bit of sport.'

'Was he an Englishman?'

'No, sir; he was a Jew. He catch a lot of foxes with some traps; he kill them and he take their skins to Jaffa to the tailor, and he tell the tailor: "Make me one big skin out of these little ones." The tailor make one thundering big fox's skin, big enough for Simpson to get inside of it. Then Simpson, he put on that skin one night, and go and sit out in the field and make the same noise what the little foxes make. The little foxes come out of their holes to look; they see one big fox sitting there, and they not know it's really Simpson. They come quite near and Simpson catch hold of their tails and tie their tails together. Then they make the noise, and still more foxes come, and Simpson catch hold of their tails and tie their tails together, till he got hundreds and hundreds.'

'Whatever did he do with them?' inquired the parson.

'He set fire to them.'

'What on earth did he do that for?'

'That, sir, was to annoy his wife's relations.'

'And would you believe it,' added Suleymân when he told me the story, 'that foolish preacher did not know that it is in the Bible. He took it all down in his notebook as the exploit of a Jewish traveller. He was the Heavy One.'

The last remark was in allusion to an Arabic proverb of which Suleymân was very fond:

'When the Heavy One alights in the territory of a people there is nothing for the inhabitants except departure.'

Which, in its turn, is an allusion to the following story:

A colony of ducks lived on an island in a river happily until a certain day, when the carcase of an ox came drifting down the current and stuck upon the forepoint of that island. They tried in vain to lift it up or push it off; it was too heavy to be moved an inch by all their efforts. They named it in their speech the Heavy One. Its stench infected the whole island, and kept on increasing until the hapless ducks were forced to emigrate.

Many Heavy Ones fell to the lot of Suleymân as dragoman, and he was by temperament ill-fitted to endure their neighbourhood. Upon the other hand, he sometimes happened on eccentrics who rejoiced his heart. An American admiral, on shore in Palestine for two days, asked only one thing: to be shown the tree on which Judas Iscariot had hanged himself, in order that he might defile it in a natural manner and so attest his faith. Suleymân was able to conduct him to the very tree, and to make the journey occupy exactly the time specified. The American was satisfied, and wrote him out a handsome testimonial.

It must have been a hardship for Suleymân—a man by nature sensitive and independent—to take his orders from some kinds of tourists and endure their rudeness. If left alone to manage the whole journey, he was—I have been told, and I can well believe it—the best guide in Syria, devoting all his energies to make the tour illuminating and enjoyable; if heckled or distrusted, he grew careless and eventually dangerous, intent to play off jokes on people whom he counted enemies. One Englishman, with a taste for management but little knowledge of the country, and no common sense, he cruelly obeyed in all things, with the natural result in loss of time and loss of luggage, sickness and discomfort. That was his way of taking vengeance on the Heavy Ones.

'And yet the man was happy, having had things his own way, even after the most horrid and disastrous journey ever made,' he told me with a sigh. 'Some men are asses.'

One afternoon, when I was riding round the bay from Akka towards the foot of Carmel, supposing Suleymân to be a hundred miles away, I came upon a group of tourists by the river Kishon, on the outskirts of the palm grove. They had alighted and were grouped around a dragoman in gorgeous raiment, like gulls around a parrot. The native of the land was holding forth to them. His voice was richly clerical in intonation, which made me notice that his audience consisted solely of members of the clergy and their patient women.

'This, ladies and gentlemen,' the rascal was declaiming like a man inspired, 'is that ancient riffer, the riffer Kishon.

It was here that the great Brophet Elijah bring the Brophets of Baal after he catch them with that dirty trick which I exblain to you about the sacrifice ub there upon that mountain what you see behind you. Elijah he come strollin' down, quite habby, to this ancient riffer, singin' one little song; and the beoble they lug down those wicked brophets. Then Elijah take one big, long knife his uncle gif him and sharben it ubon a stone like what I'm doin'. Then he gif a chuckle and he look among those brophets; and he see one man he like the look of, nice and fat; and he say: "Bring me that man!" They bring that man; Elijah slit his throat and throw him in the riffer. Then he say: "Bring his brother!" and they bring his brother, and he slit his throat and throw him in the riffer ... till they was ALL gone. Then Elijah clean his knife down in the earth, and when he'd finished laughin' he put ub a brayer.

'That was a glorious massycration, gentlemen!'

The preacher was Suleymân, at struggle with the Heavy Ones. He was not at all abashed when he caught sight of me.

LOVE AND THE PATRIARCH

I was staying for some weeks at Howard's Hotel in Jerusalem (Iskender Awwad, the dragoman, had transformed himself into the Chevalier Alexander Howard, a worthy, if choleric, gentleman, and a good friend of mine), and I rode out every day upon a decent pony, which I had discovered in the stables at the back of the hotel. One afternoon a nephew of the stable-owner, who was something of a blood, proposed that we should ride together out towards Bethlehem. His horse was a superb and showy stallion, quite beyond his power to manage properly. My modest steed was fired to emulation, and, once beyond the outskirts of Jerusalem, we tore away. At a corner where the road was narrow between rocks, I do not know exactly how, the big horse cannoned into mine and overturned him. I pitched headlong on some stones.

My first impression was that I had struck a wet spot in that arid wilderness. Then I saw my horse at a great distance, galloping, and heard the nephew of the owner saying that he must pursue it, while I must mount his horse and ride on slowly.

'Not half a mile from here, upon that hill,' he said, 'is Katamûn, the country seat of the Greek Patriarch. There you are certain to find people who will have compassion. Would God that I had never lived to see this day! Would God that I were in the grave instead of you!'

He seemed beside himself with grief and fear on my account; and yet the sense of property remained supreme. His first concern was to retrieve the runaway.

Bewildered and unable to see clearly, I did not mount the horse, which would have mastered me in that condition, but led him slowly up the hill to Katamûn. Upon the top there was a grove of trees, above which peeped some flat roofs and a dome. At length I reached the gate of this enclosure. It was open, and I led the horse along a sort of drive, on which were many chickens and a tethered sheep, which, bolting round a tree at our approach, became inextricably tangled in its rope.

In a court between a little church and other buildings, a grim old woman in a coloured head-veil looked at me out of a doorway. I called to her that I had had an accident, and asked the favour of some washing-water and a bandage. She stared at me in doleful wise, and shook her head.

'Water! Bring me water!' I insisted.

She went indoors and fetched a man of the same breed, whose eyes grew large and dull with horror at the sight of me.

Again I asked to be allowed to wash my head and face.

I heard the woman whisper: 'Shall I bring it?' and the man reply: 'Let be! This blood-stained form is half a corpse already. He will surely die. The horse, perhaps, is stolen. There has been a fight. If we should touch him we might be concerned in it. Wait till the end. Then we will summon his Beatitude, and have our testimony written down to prove our innocence.'

Amazed at their stupidity, I took a step towards them, arguing. They vanished headlong, when I realised for the first time that my appearance was in truth alarming. Perceiving the advantage that appearance gave me, I pursued them, promising them plagues in this world and perdition in the next unless they brought some water instantly.

The horse, which I was leading all this while, had been as quiet as a lamb; but, frightened by my shouts and gestures, he became unmanageable. I was struggling with him in the doorway of the house when a large and dignified ecclesiastic came upon the scene, the jewelled cross upon his cassock flashing in the sun. In the twinkling of an eye, it seemed to me, he had subdued the horse and tied him to a ring in the wall which I, in my bewilderment, had failed to see; had seized me by the collar of my coat and driven me before him through a kind of tunnel to a second court in which there was a cistern and a pump. He worked that pump and held my head beneath it, cursing the servants for a pack of imbeciles.

The man and woman reappeared, completely tamed. He sent them running, one for stuff to make a bandage, the other for medicaments, but said no word to me until the work was ended, when he grinned and asked: 'Art happy now?'

I told him that I felt a great deal better.

'Good,' he said, and led me by the hand into an upper chamber, richly carpeted, and furnished with a cushioned divan, of which the windows framed a wide view eastward over the Judæan wilderness.

There, sitting comfortably, he asked who I was and of what country; and, hearing that I came from England, questioned me about the High Church and the Low Church in that land, and whether they formed one communion or were separate—a problem which he seemed to think of great importance. He was glad, he said, that I was not a Roman Catholic, a sect which he regarded as the worst of heretics.

But his concern with all these matters seemed perfunctory compared with the delight he took in farming; for when I noticed from the window some sleek cows munching in a small enclosure, he brightened up and told me they were recent purchases. He talked about his poultry and his sheep and goats, all of which he would be pleased to show me if I cared to see them.

Accordingly, when we had drunk some coffee, which completed my revival, he took me out and showed me round his small demesne. We were standing in the shade of trees, discussing turkeys, when my companion of the road arrived upon the truant horse. He was a member of the Orthodox Greek Church.

What was my amazement when, having tied up the horse, he came with reverent haste and knelt at my companion's feet, kissing his hand with pious and devoted fervour. The grey-bearded priest, with full brown eyes, and hair that curled below the tall black head-dress like a trimming of grey *astrakhan*, with whom I had been talking so familiarly, was no other than the successor of St. James, the Orthodox Patriarch of Jerusalem. I had supposed him some sub-prior or domestic chaplain. His Beatitude acknowledged my surprise by an ironic grin.

The new arrival, still upon his knees, embarked on a long story, told in lamentable tones, about a man who was in love, and like to die of it, with a young girl who was the sister of his brother's wife. It is forbidden by the canons of the Eastern Church for two brothers to marry two sisters.

'Is there no way by which he may obtain her lawfully?' the supplicant asked.

The Patriarch assumed an air of weariness, and shook his head.

'If he were a Catholic or a Protestant he could obtain her lawfully.'

The Patriarch assumed an air of pitying scorn.

'The case is very hard,' the suppliant moaned, as he rose up from the ground at last and cleaned his knees.

The Patriarch, with a shrug, remarked that it was so. The young man should not have cast eyes upon a maid unlawful to him.

'The only way,' he said, 'is to obtain annulment of the brother's marriage by proving it to be illegal in some way.' With that he left the subject and resumed his talk concerning poultry. My companion of the road was plucking at my sleeve.

I took leave of the Patriarch respectfully, with many thanks. He clapped me on the shoulder, saying: 'Come again! And never seek to wed the sister of your brother's wife. Your Church does not forbid such marriage—does it?—being still tainted with the Latin heresy. Why does the Orthodox Church forbid it? Because it brings confusion into families, and is indecent.'

He seemed to jest, but the look he gave to my companion as we rode away was stern, I thought, and more than half-contemptuous.

Excepting that my head was bandaged, I felt well again; so we rode on, as we had first intended, towards Bethlehem. Over a rocky land with patches of pink cyclamen, black crows were wheeling in a sky of vivid blue.

We came into the olive groves beneath the hill on which stands the Greek priory of Mâr Elias, when my companion said ingratiatingly: 'If you please, we will call at the monastery and take refreshment. The monks are friends of mine. It was with the object of this visit that I led our ride in this direction.'

As I raised no objection, we tied up our horses in the garden of the monastery and went in. We found the Prior in the middle of a tea-party, a number of Greek neighbours, of both sexes, being gathered in a very comfortably-furnished room.

My friend, ere entering, implored me in a whisper not to tell them that my accident was owing to his clumsy horsemanship. Instead, he put about some story which I did not clearly overhear—something about a fight with desert Arabs, redounding to my credit, I conclude, from the solicitude which everyone expressed on my account when he had told it. Some of the ladies present insisted on a second washing of my wounds with rose-water, and a second bandaging with finer linen than the Patriarch had used. Some monks, their long hair frizzed coquettishly and tied with ribbon, helped in the work. I did not like the look of them. My friend meanwhile was talking to some pretty girls.

When we rode off again towards Jerusalem he asked me questions about the Anglican and Roman Churches, and seemed to think it a sad defect in the former that it lacked the faculty of dispensation with regard to marriage.

After a space of silence, as we were riding down the hill by the Ophthalmic Hospital, with the Tower of David and the city walls crowning the steep before us, he inquired: 'Did you observe those girls with whom I was conversing—especially the one with pale-blue ribbons. It is her I love.' And, when I complimented him on his good taste, he added: 'I think I shall become a Catholic,' and started weeping.

I then learnt from his broken speech that he was himself the hapless lover of his story to the Patriarch. The girl whom I had seen at Mâr Elias was the sister of his brother's wife. I was as sympathetic in appearance as I could be; but somehow all my sympathy was with the Patriarch, who seemed to me the only man whom I had seen that day.

THE UNPOPULAR LANDOWNER

I had decided to buy land and settle down in Syria; and had obtained consent from home upon condition that I did not spend more than a certain sum of money, not a large one, which, Suleymân had told me, would be quite sufficient for the purpose. He pointed out how lands, at present desert, and to be bought for a mere song, could be rendered profitable for the cost of bringing water to them. There was such a tract of land adjacent to the village where he had a house, with water running under it at no great depth. Rashîd, my servant, did not like this notion of converting deserts into gardens. He called it simple waste of time and labour, when gardens readymade were going cheap. There was a nice estate, with two perennial springs within its boundaries, near his village in the north. His people would be proud and gratified if I would honour their poor dwelling while inspecting it. Suleymân lamented that his house was quite unworthy of my occupation, but proposed to have a fine pavilion pitched outside it, if I would deign to grace the village as his guest.

'Depend upon it,' said an Englishman whom I consulted on one of my rare visits to the city, 'the land they recommend belongs to their relations. They will sell it you for twenty times the market value, and then adhere to you like leeches till they've sucked you dry.' He added: 'I advise you to give up the whole idea,' but I was used to that advice, and firm against it.

His warning against native counsellors, however, weighed with me to this extent, that I determined to ignore the lands they recommended in their neighbourhood. Each was at first cast down when I announced this resolution. But presently Rashîd exclaimed: 'No matter where we dwell. I still shall serve you'; and Suleymân, after smoking his *narghîleh* a long while in silence, said: 'Each summer I will visit you and give advice.'

All three of us then set to work upon inquiries. Innumerable were the *sheykhs* who seemed to be in money difficulties and wished to sell their land. Some owners journeyed forty miles to come and see me, and explain the great advantage of their property. But, knowing something of the Land Code, I inquired about the tenure. I wanted only 'mulk' or freehold land; and *'wakf'* (land held in tail or mortmain) of various and awful kinds is much more common. At last a *sheykh* came who declared his land was *'mulk,'* and certain of our neighbours, men of worth, testified of their certain knowledge that he spoke the truth.

The village where the property was situated was a long day's journey from our own. A fortnight after my discussion with the owner Suleymân and I set out on our way thither, having sent Rashîd ahead of us to find a decent lodging, since it was our intention to remain there several days.

The village was arranged in steps upon a mountain side, the roofs of houses on the lower level serving as approach to those above. On all the steep slopes round about it there were orchards, with now and then a flat-roofed house among the trees.

Rashîd came out to meet us, accompanied by certain of the elders, among whom I looked in vain for the owner of the land we were to visit. My first inquiry was for him. Rashîd replied: 'He is unpopular. I went to the chief people of the village'—he waved his hand towards the persons who escorted him—'and they have set apart a house and stable for your Honour's use.'

The house turned out to be a single room, cube-shaped, and furnished only with some matting. The stable, part of the same building, was exactly like it, except that it was open at one end.

We had our supper at a tavern by the village spring, surrounded by a friendly crowd of *fellâhîn*. Again I looked for the old gentleman whom I had come to see, and whispered my surprise at not beholding him. Rashîd again replied: 'He is unpopular.'

Returning to the house with me, Rashîd arranged my bed; put candle, matches, cigarettes within my reach; fastened the shutters of two windows; and retired, informing me that he and Suleymân were sleeping at the dwelling of the headman of the place.

I had got into my bed upon the floor when there came a knocking on the solid wooden shutters which Rashîd had closed. I went and opened one of them a little way. It was moonlight, but the window looked into the gloom of olive trees. A voice out of the shadows questioned:

'Is it thou, the Englishman?'

It was the owner of the land, who then reproached me in heartbroken tones because I had not let him know the hour of my arrival, that he and his three sons might have gone forth upon the road to meet me. The owners of the place where now I lodged were his chief enemies. He begged me to steal forth at once and come with him. When I refused, he groaned despairingly and left me with the words:

'Believe not anything they say about us or the property.'

I closed the shutter and went back to bed. But it was hot. I rose again and opened both the windows so as to secure whatever breeze there was, and, after a long spell of angry tossing due to sandflies, fell asleep. When I awoke the room was full of daylight and a murmur which I first mistook for that of insects, but soon found out to be the voice of a considerable crowd of human beings. At every window was a press of faces and of women's head-veils, and children raised upon their mothers' shoulders. I heard a child's sad wail: 'O mother, lift me up that I, too, may behold the unbeliever!'

I made haste to cover myself somehow, for in my sleep I had kicked off the bedclothes, and commanded all those women to be gone immediately. They merely grinned and wished me a good day, and then discussed my personal appearance, the whiteness of my skin, and more particularly my pyjamas, with much interest. This went on till Rashîd appeared upon the scene, bringing my india-rubber bath and a kerosene tin full of water. He closed and bolted all the shutters firmly, with stern reflections on the lack of shame of my admirers.

I told him of the visit of the owner of the land.

He answered as before: 'He is unpopular.'

I asked the reason, and he told me:

'There are in this part of the country two factions which have existed from old time. All the people in this village are adherents of one faction, except that old man and his children, who uphold the other. The people would not mind so much if he kept silent, but he gibes at them and vaunts his party upon all occasions. They intend to kill him. That is why he wants to sell. It is good to know this, since it gives us an advantage.'

Suleymân arrived. We all three breakfasted on slabs of country bread and a great bowl of curds, and then went out to view that old man's land. The *sheykh*—whose name was Yûsuf—and his sons were there to show us round, and, though the property was not extensive, they contrived to keep us there till noon, when a round meal was spread for us beneath some trees. And after that was finished, the *sheykh* availed himself of some remark of mine to start the whole perambulation once again.

At last it came to mention of the price, which seemed to me excessive, and I said so to my friends.

Rashîd replied: 'Of course! The business has not yet begun. Tomorrow and the next day we shall view the land again; and after that we shall arrange for the appointment of two valuers, one for us and one for him, who will inspect the land, first separately, then together; and after that we shall appoint an arbiter who will remonstrate with the owner of the land; and after that——'

'But the business will take months.'

'That is the proper way, unless your Honour wishes to be cheated.'

'What is your opinion?' I inquired of Suleymân.

'The land is good, and capable of much improvement,' he replied, 'and all the trees go with it, which is an advantage. Also the source of water will be all our own.'

Suleymân repeated this remark in presence of the crowd of villagers whom we found awaiting our return before my house. At once there rose a cry: 'That Yûsuf is a liar. Some of the trees do not belong to him. The water, too, does not originate upon his property, but on the hill above, so can be cut from him.'

Suleymân was talking with the village headman. When he returned to me his face was grave.

'What is it?' I inquired. 'Has the *Sheykh* Yûsuf been deceiving us?'

He shook his head with a disgusted frown before replying:

'No, it is these others who are lying through dislike of him. Is your heart set upon the purchase of that land?'

'By no means.'

'That is good; because this village is a nest of hornets. The headman has long marked that land out for his own. Were we to pay *Sheykh* Yûsuf a good price for it, enabling him to leave the neighbourhood with honour, they would hate us and work for our discomfort in a multitude of little ways. We will call upon the *Sheykh* tomorrow and cry off the bargain, because your Honour caught a touch of fever from the land today. That is a fair excuse.'

We proffered it upon the morrow, when the *Sheykh* Yûsuf received it with a scarce veiled sneer, seeming extremely mortified. Directly after we had left him, we heard later, he went down to the tavern by the village spring and cursed the elders who had turned my mind against him in unmeasured terms; annoying people so that they determined there and then to make an end of him.

Next morning, when we started on our homeward way, there was a noise of firing in the village, and, coming round a shoulder of the hill in single file we saw *Sheykh* Yûsuf seated on a chair against the wall of his house, and screened by a great olive tree, the slits in whose old trunk made perfect loopholes, blazing away at a large crowd of hostile *fellâhîn*. He used, in turn, three rifles, which his sons kept loading for him. He was seated, as we afterwards found out, because he had been shot in the leg.

I was for dashing to his rescue, and Rashîd was following.

We should both have lost our lives, most probably, if Suleymân had not shouted at that moment, in stentorian tones: 'Desist, in the name of the Sultan and all the Powers of Europe! Desist, or every one of you shall surely hang!'

Such words aroused the people's curiosity. The firing ceased while we rode in between them and their object; and Suleymân assured the villagers politely that I was the right hand and peculiar agent of the English Consul-General, with absolutely boundless power to hang and massacre.

Upon the other hand, we all three argued with *Sheykh* Yûsuf that he should leave the place at once and lay his case before the Governor.

'We will go with him,' said Suleymân to me, 'in order that your Honour may be made acquainted with the Governor—a person whom you ought to know. His property will not be damaged in his absence, for they fear the law. The heat of war is one thing, and cold-blooded malice is another. It is the sight and sound of him that irritates them and so drives them to excess.'

At length we got the *Sheykh* on horseback and upon the road; but he was far from grateful, wishing always to go back and fight. We could not get a civil word from him on the long ride, and just before we reached the town where lived the Governor he managed to escape.

Rashîd flung up his hands when we first noticed his defection. 'No wonder that he is unpopular,' he cried disgustedly. 'To flee from us, his benefactors, after we have come so far out of our way through kindness upon his account. It is abominable. Who, under Allah, could feel love for such a man?'

THE CAÏMMACÂM

Though the reason of our coming, the *Sheykh* Yûsuf, had deserted us, we rode into the town and spent the night there, finding lodgings at a *khan* upon the outskirts of the place, of which the yard was shaded by a fine old carob tree. While we were having breakfast the next morning in a kind of gallery which looked into the branches of that tree, and through them and a ruined archway to the road, crowded just then with peasants in grey clothing coming in to market, Suleymân proposed that he and I should go and call upon the Caïmmacâm, the local Governor. I had spent a wretched night. The place was noisy and malodorous. My one desire was to be gone as soon as possible, and so I answered:

'I will call on no one. My only wish to see him was upon account of that old rogue who ran away from us.'

'The man was certainly ungrateful—curse his father!' said Rashîd.

'The man is to be pitied, being ignorant,' said Suleymân. 'His one idea was to defend his house and land by combat. He did not perceive that by the course of law and influence he might defend them more effectually, and forever. He probably did not imagine that your Honour would yourself approach the Governor and plead with him.'

'I shall see nobody,' I answered crossly. 'We return at once.'

'Good,' said Rashîd. 'I get the horses ready.'

'And yet,' said our preceptor thoughtfully, 'his Excellency

is, they say, a charming man; and this would be a golden opportunity for us to get acquainted with him and bespeak his favour. Thus the *Sheykh* Yûsuf, though himself contemptible, may be of service to us. Already I have told the people here that we have come on an important errand to the Governor. Rashîd, too, as I know, has spoken of the matter in a boastful way. If, after that, we should depart in dudgeon without seeing him, there would be gossip and perhaps—God knows—even political disturbance. The Governor, coming to hear of it, might reasonably feel aggrieved.'

He argued so ridiculously, yet so gravely, that in the end I was obliged to yield. And so, a little before ten o'clock, we sauntered through the narrow streets to the Government offices—a red-roofed, whitewashed building near which soldiers loitered, in a dusty square.

There we waited for a long while in an ante-room—spacious, but rather dingy, with cushionless divans around the walls, on which a strange variety of suitors sat or squatted. Some of these appeared so poor that I admired their boldness in demanding audience of the Governor. Yet it was one of the most wretched in appearance who was called first by the turbaned, black-robed usher. He passed into an inner room: the door was shut.

Then Suleymân went over to the usher, who kept guard upon that door, and held a whispered conversation with him. I know not what he said; but, when the wretched-looking man came out again, the usher slipped into the inner room with reverence and, presently returning, bowed to us and bade us enter. I went in, followed by Suleymân, who swelled and strutted like a pouter pigeon in his flowing robes.

The *Caïmmacâm* was a nice-looking Turk of middle-age,

extremely neat in his apparel and methodical in his surroundings. He might have been an Englishman but for the crimson *fez* upon his brow and a chaplet of red beads, with which he toyed perpetually. He gazed into my eyes with kind inquiry. I told him that I came with tidings of a grave disturbance in his district, and then left Suleymân to tell the story of *Sheykh* Yûsuf and his neighbours and the battle we had witnessed in the olive grove before his house.

Suleymân exhausted all his powers of language and of wit, making a veritable poem of the episode. The Governor did not appear profoundly interested.

'*Sheykh* Yûsuf! Who is he?' he asked at the conclusion of the tale.

I explained that the *Sheykh* Yûsuf was a landowner, whose acquaintance we had made through my desire to buy some property.

'Your Honour thinks of settling here among us?' cried his Excellency, with sudden zest, appearing quite enraptured with the notion. He asked then if the French tongue was intelligible to me, and, hearing that it was, talked long in French about my project, which seemed to please him greatly. He said that it would be a blessing for his district to have a highly civilised, enlightened being like myself established in it as the sun and centre of improvement; and what a comfort it would be to him particularly to have an educated man at hand to talk to! He hoped that, when I had set up my model farm—for a model it would be, in every way, he felt quite sure of that, from my appearance and my conversation—I would not limit my attention solely to the work of agriculture, but would go on to improve the native breeds of sheep and oxen. He heard that splendid strains of both were found in England. He wished me to import a lot of English bulls

and rams, assuring me of the assistance of the
Government in all that I might do in that direction, since
the Sultan ('His Imperial Majesty' he called him always)
took the greatest interest in such experiments.

All this was very far from my original design, which was
to lead as far as possible a quiet life. But I promised to give
thought to all his Excellency's counsels.

He made me smoke two cigarettes and drink a cup of
coffee which his secretary had prepared upon a brazier in a
corner of the room; and then, with a sweet smile and
deprecating gestures of the hands, he begged me to excuse
him if he closed the interview. It was a grief to him to let
me go, but he was very busy.

I rose at once, and so did Suleymân.

'But what of the *Sheykh* Yûsuf?' I exclaimed, reminding
him.

'Ah, to be sure!' rejoined the Governor with a slight
frown. 'Of what religion is he?'

'I suppose a *Druze*.'

'And the people who attacked him so unmercifully?'

'Are *Druzes* too.'

'Ah, then, it is all in the family, as the saying goes. And,
unless some deputation from the *Druze* community appeals
to me, I should be ill-advised to interfere in its affairs. Our
way of government is not identical with that which is
pursued with such conspicuous success in highly civilised
and settled countries like your own. We leave the various
communities and tribes alone to settle their internal
differences. It is only where tribe wars on tribe, religion on
religion, or their quarrels stop the traffic on the Sultan's
highway that we intervene. What would you have, *mon ami*?
We are here in Asia!'

With these words, and a smile of quite ineffable indulgence for my young illusions, his Excellency bowed me out.

In the ante-room Suleymân drew close to my left ear and whispered sharply:

'Give me four *mejîdîs*.'

'Whatever for?' I asked in deep amazement.

'That I will tell you afterwards. The need is instant.'

I produced the four *mejîdîs* from a trouser-pocket, and, receiving them, he went back to the door by which the usher stood, and whispered to the man, who went inside a moment and came back with the private secretary of the *Caïmmacâm*. The compliments which passed between them seemed to me interminable.

I paced the pavement of the waiting-room, the only figure in the crowd whose attitude bespoke impatience. The others sat or squatted round the walls in perfect resignation, some of them smoking, others munching nuts of various kinds, of which the shells began to hide the floor adjacent to them. A few of the suppliants had even had the forethought to bring with them bags full of provisions, as if anticipating that their time of waiting might endure for several days.

At last, when I was growing really angry with him, Suleymân returned and told me:

'All is well, and we can now be going, if your Honour pleases.'

'I do please,' I rejoined indignantly. 'Why have you kept me waiting all this while? I never wished to come at all into this place, and Allah knows that we have done no good by coming. We have spoilt a morning which we might have spent upon the road.'

'Allah, Allah!' sighed Suleymân long-sufferingly. 'Your Honour is extremely hard to please. Did not his Excellency talk to you exclusively, with every sign of the most lively pleasure for quite half an hour; whereas he scarcely deigned to throw a word to me, although I wooed his ear with language calculated to seduce the mind of kings? I have some cause to be dejected at neglect from one so powerful; but you have every cause to be elated. He is now your friend.'

'I shall never see him in my life again most likely!' I objected.

'Nay, that you cannot tell,' replied my mentor suavely. 'To be acquainted with a person in authority is always well.'

CONCERNING BRIBES

'Why did you want those four *mejîdis?*' I inquired severely.

Suleymân shrugged up his shoulders and replied:

'I had to pay the proper fees, since you yourself showed not a sign of doing so, to save our carefully established honour and good name.'

'You don't mean that you gave them to the *Caïmmacâm?*'

'Allah forbid! Consider, O beloved, my position in this matter. To put it in the form of parables: Suppose a king and his *vizier* should pay a visit to another king and his *vizier*. If there were presents to be made, I ask you, would not those intended for the king be offered personally by the king, and those for the *vizier* by the *vizier?* It will be obvious to your Honour, upon slight reflection, that if, in our adventure of this morning, a present to the Governor was necessary or desirable, you personally, and no other creature, should have made it.'

'Merciful Allah!' I exclaimed. 'He would have knocked me down.'

'He would have done nothing of the kind, being completely civilised. He would merely have pushed back your hand with an indulgent smile, pressing it tenderly, as who should say: "you are a child in these things, and do not know our ways, being a stranger." Yet, undoubtedly, upon the whole, your offer of a gift, however small, would have confirmed the good opinion which he formed at sight of you.

'But let that pass! Out of the four *mejîdis* which you gave

134

me so reluctantly (since you ask for an account) I presented one to the usher, and three to his Excellency's private secretary, in your name. And I have procured it of the secretary's kindness that he will urge his lord to take some measures to protect that ancient malefactor, the *Sheykh* Yûsuf.'

'If I had tipped the Governor, as you suggest that I ought to have done,' I interrupted vehemently, 'do you mean to say he would have taken measures to protect *Sheykh* Yûsuf?'

'Nay, I say not that; but he would at least have had complete conviction that your Honour takes a lively interest in that old churl—a person in himself unpleasant and unworthy of a single thought from any thinking or right-minded individual. Thus, even though he scorned the money, as he would no doubt have done, the offer would have told him we were earnest in our application, and he might conceivably have taken action from desire to do a pleasure to one whom, as I said before, he loved at sight.'

'The whole system is corrupt,' I said, 'and what is worse, unreasonable.'

'So say the Franks,' replied Suleymân, shrugging his shoulders up and spreading wide his hands, as though before a wall of blind stupidity which he knew well could never be cast down nor yet surmounted. 'Our governors, our judges, and the crowd of small officials are not highly paid, and what they do receive is paid irregularly. Then all, whether high or low, must live; and it is customary in our land to offer gifts to persons in authority, because a smile, God knows, is always better than a frown from such an one. We are not like the Franks, who barter everything, even their most sacred feelings, even love. It gives us pleasure to make gifts, and see them welcomed, even when the recipient is someone who cannot in any way repay us for our trouble, as a Frank would say.'

'But to sell justice; for it comes to that!' I cried, indignant.

'Who talks of selling justice? You are quite mistaken. If I have to go before a judge I make a gift beforehand to his Honour, whose acceptance tells me, not that he will give a verdict in my favour—do not think it!—but merely that his mind contains no grudge against me. If he refused the gift I should be terrified, since I should think he had been won completely by the other side. To take gifts from both parties without preference, making allowance, when there is occasion, for the man who is too poor to give; and then to judge entirely on the merits of the case; that is the way of upright judges in an Eastern country. The gifts we make are usually small, whereas the fees which lawyers charge in Western countries are exorbitant, as you yourself have told me more than once and I have heard from others. And even after paying those enormous fees, the inoffensive, righteous person is as like to suffer as the guilty. Here, for altogether harmless men to suffer punishment in place of rogues is quite unheard-of; though occasionally one notorious evildoer may be punished for another's crime when this is great and the real criminal cannot be found and there is call for an example to be made upon the instant. This generally happens when a foreign consul interferes, demanding vengeance for some slight offence against his nationals. Things like that take place occasionally when the court is flustered. But in its natural course, believe me, Turkish justice, if slow-moving, is as good as that of Europe and infinitely less expensive than your English law.'

I made no answer, feeling quite bewildered.

Suleymân was always serious in manner, which made it

very hard to tell when he was joking or in earnest. Among the natives of the land, I knew, he had the reputation of a mighty joker, but I had learnt the fact from the applause of others. I never should have guessed from his demeanour that he jested consciously.

He also held his peace until we reached our hostelry. There, some half-hour later, when I had given orders for our horses to be ready for a start directly after luncheon—a decision against which Suleymân protested unsuccessfully, declaring it would be too hot for riding—I overheard him telling the whole story of our visit, including the donation of the four *mejîdis*, to Rashîd, who was lazily engaged in polishing my horse's withers.

'That secretary is a man of breeding,' he was saying, in a tone of warm approval; 'for I noticed he was careful to receive the present in his left hand, which he placed behind his back in readiness, with great decorum. Nor did he thank me, or give any token of acknowledgment beyond a little friendly twinkle of the eyes.'

At once I pounced on this admission, crying: 'That shows that he regarded the transaction as unlawful! And your remark upon it shows that you, too, think it so.'

Suleymân looked slowly round until his eyes met mine, not one whit disconcerted, though until I spoke he had not known that I was anywhere in earshot.

'Your Honour is incorrigible,' he replied, with a grave smile. 'I never knew your like for obstinacy in a false opinion; which shows that you were born to fill some high position in the world. Of course they all—these fine officials, great and small—regard it as beneath their dignity to take a present which they sorely need. To take such presents greedily would be to advertise their poverty to all the world. And Government appointments swell a man with pride, if nothing else—a pride which makes them anxious to be thought above all fear of want. For that cause, they are half-ashamed of taking gifts. But no one in this country thinks it wrong of them to do so, nor to oblige the giver, if they can, in little ways. It would be wrong if they betrayed the trust reposed in them by their superiors, or were seduced into some act against their loyalty or their religion. But that, praise be to God, you will not find. It is only in small matters such as acts of commerce or politeness, which hardly come within the sphere of a man's conscience, that they are procurable, and no one in this country thinks the worse of them, whatever people say to you, a foreigner, by way of flattery. It is very difficult for foreigners to learn the truth. Your Honour should be thankful that you have Suleymân for an instructor—and Rashîd, too,' he added as an after-thought, seeing that my bodyservant stood close by, expecting mention.

And after more than twenty years' experience of Eastern matters, I know now that he was right.

The Battlefield

Our road, the merest bridle-path, which sometimes altogether disappeared and had to be retrieved by guesswork, meandered on the side of a ravine, down in the depths of which, in groves of oleander, there flowed a stream of which we caught the murmur. The forest was continuous on our side of the *wadi*. It consisted of dense olive groves around the villages and a much thinner growth of ilex in the tracts between. The shade was pleasant in the daytime, but as night came on its gloom oppressed our spirits with extreme concern, for we were still a long way off our destination, and uncertain of the way.

The gloom increased. From open places here and there we saw the stars, but gloom filled the ravine, and there was little difference between the darkness underneath the trees and that outside in open spaces of the grove. We trusted to our horses to make out the path, which sometimes ran along the verge of precipices.

I cannot say that I was happy in my mind. Rashîd made matters worse by dwelling on the risks we ran not only from abandoned men but ghouls and *jinnis*. The lugubrious call of a hyæna in the distance moved him to remark that ghouls assume that shape at night to murder travellers. They come up close and rub against them like a loving cat; which contact robs the victims of their intellect, and causes them to follow the hyæna to its den, where the ghoul kills them and inters their bodies till the flesh is ripe.

He next expressed a fear lest we might come upon some

ruin lighted up, and be deceived into supposing it a haunt
of men, as had happened to a worthy cousin of his own
when on a journey. This individual, whose name was Ali,
had been transported in the twinkling of an eye by *jinnis*,
from somewhere in the neighbourhood of Hamá to the
wilds of Jebel Câf (Mount Caucasus), and had escaped a
hideous and painful death only by recollection of the name
of God. He told me, too, how he himself, when stationed
at Mersîn, had met a company of demons, one fine evening
in returning from an errand; and other tales which caused
my flesh to creep.

The groves receded. We were in an open place where
only a low kind of brushwood grew, when suddenly my
horse shied, gave a fearful snort, and sturdily refused to
budge another inch. I let him stand until Rashîd came up.
He thought to pass me, but his horse refused as mine had
done.

'It is no doubt some *jinni* in the way,' he whispered in a
frightened tone; then, calling out: '*Dastûr, ya mubârak*'
(Permission, blessed one!), he tried to urge his horse, which
still demurred. So there we were, arrested by some unseen
hand; and this became the more unpleasant because a
pestilential smell was in the place.

'Better return!' muttered Rashîd, with chattering teeth.

'Give me a match!' I said distractedly. 'My box is empty.'

'Better return!' he pleaded.

'A match, do you hear?' I cried, made cross by terror.

He gave the match, and I believe I shouted as I struck it.
For a brief space it made a dazzle in my eyes, preventing
me from seeing anything, and then went out.

'There is something lying in the path!' Rashîd was
gibbering.

I got down off my horse and lit a second match, which I took care to shelter till the flame was strong. A human arm lay in the path before us.

My horror was extreme, and grew uncanny when the match expired. But the ghastly object had restored his courage to Rashîd, who even laughed aloud as he exclaimed:

'The praise to Allah! It is nothing which can hurt us. No doubt some murder has been here committed, all unknown. The Lord have mercy on the owner of that arm! We will report the matter to some high official at our journey's end.'

We turned our horses to the right and made a long detour, but scarcely had they found the path again when mine (which led the way) demurred once more.

'Another piece,' exclaimed Rashîd excitedly. He got down off his horse to look. 'Nay, many pieces. This, by Allah, is no other than a battlefield unknown to fame.'

'How can a battle take place without public knowledge?' I inquired, incredulous.

'The thing may happen when two factions quarrel for unlawful cause—it may be over stolen gains, or for some deadly wrong which cannot be avowed without dishonour—and when each side exterminates the other.'

'How can that happen?' I exclaimed again.

Rashîd could not at once reply, because in our avoidance of those human relics we found ourselves on broken ground and among trunks of trees, which called for the address of all our wits. But when the horses once more plodded steadily, he assured me that the thing could happen, and had happened often in that country, where men's blood is hot. He told me how a band of brigands once, in Anti-Lebanon, had fought over their spoils till the majority on both sides had been slain, and the survivors were so badly wounded that they could not move, but lay and died upon the battlefield; and how the people of two villages, both men and women, being mad with envy, had held a battle with the same result. I interrupted him with questions. Both of us were glad to talk in order to get rid of the remembrance of our former fear. We gave the rein to our imaginations, speaking eagerly.

Reverting to the severed limbs which we had seen, Rashîd exclaimed:

'Now I will tell your Honour how it happened. A deadly insult had been offered to a family in a young girl's dishonour. Her father and her brothers killed her to wipe out the shame—as is the custom here among the *fellâhîn*—and then with all their relatives waylaid the men of the insulter's house when these were cutting wood here in the forest. There was a furious battle, lasting many hours. The combatants fought hand-to-hand with rustic weapons, and in some cases tore each other limb from limb. When all was done, the victors were themselves so sorely wounded that they were able to do nothing but lie down and die.'

'How many do you think there were?' I asked, believing.

'To judge by scent alone, not one or two; but, Allah knows, perhaps a hundred!' said Rashîd reflectively.

'It is strange they should have lain there undiscovered.'

'Not strange, when one remembers that the spot is far from any village and probably as far from the right road,' was his reply.

This last conjecture was disquieting; but we were both too much excited for anxiety.

'It is an event to be set down in histories,' Rashîd

exclaimed. 'We shall be famous people when we reach the village. Such news is heard but once in every hundred years.'

'I wish that we could reach that village,' was my answer; and again we fell to picturing the strange event.

At length we heard the barking of a dog in the far distance, and gave praise to Allah. A half-hour later we saw lights ahead of us. But that did not mean that the village was awake, Rashîd explained to me, for among the people of that country 'to sleep without a light' is to be destitute. A little later, Rashîd hammered at a door, while savage dogs bayed round us, making rushes at his heels.

'Awake, O sons of honour!' was his cry. 'A great calamity!' And, when the door was opened, he detailed the story of an awful fight, in which both parties of belligerents had been exterminated. 'They are torn limb from limb. We saw the relics,' he explained. 'If you have any doubt, question my lord who is out here behind me—a great one of the English, famed for his veracity.'

And I was ready to confirm each word he said.

In a very little while that village was astir.

It was the seat of a *mudîr* who had two soldiers at his beck and call. The great man was aroused from sleep; he questioned us, and, as the result of the inquiry, sent the soldiers with us to survey the battlefield. A crowd of peasants, armed with quarter-staves and carrying lanterns, came with the party out of curiosity. Our horses having had enough of travel, we went back on foot amid the noisy crowd, who questioned us incessantly about the strange event. The murmur of our going filled the wood and echoed from the rocks above. By the time we reached the place where we had seen the human limbs, the dawn was up, to make our lanterns useless.

Rashîd and I were certain of the spot. We came upon it with a thrill of apprehension.

But there was nothing there.

'I seek refuge in Allah!' gasped Rashîd in pious awe. 'I swear by my salvation it was here we saw them. The name of God be round about us! It is devilry.'

Our escort was divided in opinion, some thinking we had been indeed the sport of devils, others that we lied. But someone sniffed and said:

'There is a smell of death.'

There was no doubt about the smell at any rate. Then one of the *mudîr's* two soldiers, searching in the brushwood, cried: 'I have the remnant of an arm.'

And then an old man of the village smote his leg and cried:

'O my friends, I see it! Here is neither lies nor devilry.'

Laughing, he seized me by the arm and bade me come with him. We went a little way into the wood, and there he showed me three Druze tombs deep in the shade of ilex trees—small buildings made of stone and mud, like little houses, each with an opening level with the ground, and a much smaller opening, like a window, at the height of a man's elbow.

'You see?' cried my tutor. 'Those are graves. The openings on the ground were made too large, and jackals have got in and pulled the bodies out. The men who made those graves are foolish people, who have wandered from the truth. They think the spirits of the dead have need of food and light, and also of a hole for crawling in and out. I heard you ask your servant for a match just now. Come, I will show you where to find one always.'

He led me to the nearest tomb, and thrust my hand into the little hole which served as window. It touched a heap of matches which he bade me take and put into my pocket, saying:

'It is not a theft, for the matches have been thrown away, as you might say. Those foolish people will suppose the dead have struck them. They used to put wax candles and tinder-boxes with them in the niches, but when these sulphur matches came in fashion, they preferred them for economy. When I am working in this wood I take no fire with me, being quite sure to find the means of lighting one. Praise be to Allah for some people's folly!'

I thanked him for the wrinkle, and went back to join Rashîd, who was exclaiming with the others over our deception. But everyone agreed that the mistake was natural for men bewildered in the darkness of the night.

MURDERERS

Rashîd and I were riding down to Tripoli, and had long been looking for a certain *'kheymah'* or refreshment booth beside the road, which an enterprising Christian of that town had opened in the summer months for the relief of travellers. When at length we came in sight of it, we saw a crowd of men reposing on the ground before its awning. We soon lost sight of them again in a ravine, and it was not till we were close upon them, climbing up the other bank, that I remarked that most of them were shackled and in the charge of a small guard of Turkish soldiers.

'Criminals upon their way to the hard labour prison,' said Rashîd.

'What have they done?' I asked, as we dismounted.

He strolled across and put a question to their escort, then returned and told me:

'They are murderers.'

After that information it surprised me, while we ate our luncheon, to observe their open faces, and to hear them laugh and chatter with their guards. Already I had learnt that crime in Eastern countries is not regarded altogether as it is with us; that Orientals do not know that shrinking from contamination which marks the Englishman's behaviour towards a breaker of his country's law. But I was unprepared for this indulgence towards a gang of murderers. It interested me; and, seeing that Rashîd was talking with them in a friendly way, I gathered there was nothing to be feared from their proximity, and myself drew

146

near when I had finished eating, and gave them cigarettes. They thanked me loudly. The smile of pleasure on each face expressed a childlike innocence. One only sat apart in gloom, conforming in some measure to my preconceived idea of what a murderer upon his way to prison ought to look like. I noticed with surprise that this one wore no chain. I went and touched him on the shoulder. It was only then that he looked up and saw that I was wishing him to take a cigarette. He did so quickly, and saluted me without a word.

One of the others said in tender tones:

'Blame him not, O my lord, for he is mad with sorrow. He is more luckless than the rest of us—may Allah help him! He killed the person he loved best on earth—his only brother.'

'Then it is true that you are murderers?' I asked, still half-incredulous.

'By Allah, it is true, alas! and we are paying for it by a year's enslavement.'

'A year! No more than that,' I cried, 'for killing men?'

'And is it not enough, O lord of kindness? It is not as if we had killed men from malice or desire of gain. We killed in sudden anger, or, in the case of three among us, in a faction-fight. It is from Allah; and we ask forgiveness.'

'How did that man kill?' I questioned, pointing to the apathetic figure of the fratricide, which attracted my imagination by its loneliness.

'He suffered persecutions from a rich man of his village, who was his rival for the favour of a certain girl—so it is said. Those persecutions maddened him at times. One day when he was mad like that, his brother came to him and spoke some word of blame upon another matter. He killed him, as he might have killed his wife and children or himself, being in that state of mind devoid of reason. When he awoke and saw what he had done, he wished to kill himself.'

'It is from Allah! His remorse is punishment,' exclaimed Rashîd. 'Why should he go to prison? He has had enough.'

'Nobody of this country would have thought of punishment for him,' replied the spokesman of the murderers, with rueful smile. 'But his brother was the servant of a foreign merchant—a Greek from overseas, I think it was—who put the business in his Consul's hands, and so——' The speaker clicked his thumbnail on his white front teeth to signify finality. 'But the poor man himself does not object; it seems indeed that he is glad to go with us. Perhaps by labour and harsh treatment he may be relieved.'

As there were still provisions in our saddle-bags, Rashîd, by my command, divided them among the company, the soldiers and the murderers alike, who were delighted. It was a merry party which we left behind, with the exception of the fratricide, who ate the food, when it was set before him, ravenously, but said not a word.

'May Allah heal him!' sighed the other murderers. 'Our Lord remove this shadow from his mind!'

Rashîd and I pursued our way on an interminable path meandering in zig-zags down through brushwood, which smelt sweet of myrtle and wild incense. I tried to make him understand that he had quite misled me by the term he had applied to men who had been guilty of no more than manslaughter. The distinction had to be explained with much periphrasis, because the Arabic word 'Câtil' means a slayer, and is given indiscriminately to all who kill.

He caught my meaning sooner than I had expected.

'Ah!' he said. 'Your Honour thought from what I said that they were *"cutters of the road,"* (highwaymen) or hired assassins, who kill men for gain. Those are the greater criminals, whose punishment is death. Few such exist among us. Here a robber will seldom kill a man unless that man kills him.' [I translate literally] *'when it is just retaliation*; and as for hired assassins, I have known several of them in my time, and they are not bad people, but unfortunate, having fallen early in the power of cruel and ambitious men. Most of the killing in this country is done without a thought, in anger or mad jealousy.'

'Is it for man to judge them?' he exclaimed, with a high shrug, when I remarked upon their friendly treatment by the Turkish guards. 'They are punished by authority down here, so we are better; but afterwards, when comes the Judgment of the Lord, we may be worse. It is hard upon those men we met just now. They go to prison, most of them, because they were not rich enough to pay the sum demanded as the price of blood. For men of wealth, or who have rich relations, it is easy to compound the matter for a sum of money, in return for which the dead man's relatives regard his death as due to natural causes, and forswear revenge. It is hard, I say, upon those men we met just now; and especially upon the man who slew his brother—may Our Lord console him!'

A few days later I was strolling in the town and happened to pass by the public gaol. In the middle of the gate, behind some iron bars, a wretched man stood shaking a tin can, in which some small coins rattled, and calling on the passers-by for alms for the poor prisoners. A little group of English tourists—a gentleman and two fair ladies—came that way, led on by a resplendent dragoman. They stared at the wild figure at the prison gate.

'You like to give a trifle to the brisoners?' inquired the guide.

'What are they in for?' asked the gentleman.

'Murders, I guess, mostly,' shrugged the dragoman.

'Certainly not,' replied the gentleman, with indignation.

I ventured to approach and tell him that they were not murderers in our sense of the word, and that they depended for a bare subsistence upon public charity. The only thanks I got were a cold stare from the man, a fastidious grimace from the two ladies, and an 'Oh, indeed!' so arrogant in tone that I retired discomfited. My ill-success may be attributable to the fact that I was wearing a 'kufiyeh' and 'acâl' and so appeared to them as what is called a 'native.'

I myself have always, since that day, felt it my duty to give alms to murderers in Eastern lands.

THE TREES ON THE LAND

My search for an estate provided us with an excuse for visiting all sorts of out-of-the-way places, and scraping acquaintance with all sorts of curious people. In some villages we were greeted with unbounded glee; in others with a sullen, gruff endurance far from welcome. But, though the flavour of reception varied, we were everywhere received with some degree of hospitality, and shown what we desired to see. Thus we surveyed a great variety of properties, none of which fulfilled my chief requirements. I wanted both a house in which I should not feel ashamed to live, and cultivable land enough to yield a revenue; and the two together seemed impossible to find, at least for the sum of money which was placed at my disposal.

One piece of land attracted us so much that we remained in the adjacent village a full week, returning every day to wander over it, trying to see if it could not be made to fit my needs. It consisted of a grove of fine old olive trees, with terraces of fig and mulberry trees and vegetables, spread out to catch the morning sun upon a mountain side sloping to a wooded valley walled by rocky heights. Water was there in plenty, but no house to speak of; the three small, cube-shaped houses on the property being in the occupation (which amounts to ownership) of workers of the land, who, according to the custom of the country, would become my partners. Upon the other hand, the land was fairly cheap, and after paying for it, I should have a balance with which I might begin to build a proper house; for, as Suleymân remarked, 'here all things are done gradually. No one will expect to see a palace all at once.

Begin with two rooms and a stable, and add a fresh room every time that you have forty pounds to spare.'

The price of building appeared fixed in all that countryside at forty pounds a vault, which in ordinary buildings means a room, since every room is vaulted.

The trouble was to see just where to put the house without encroaching upon profitable land. At last I hit on a position in the middle of the highest terrace on which grew olive trees so very old that they could well be sacrificed. Having arrived at this decision I sat down among those trees and gazed in rapture at the view across the valley. It was indeed a grand position for a house.

Rashîd exclaimed: 'Our dwelling will be seen afar. The traveller on distant roads will see its windows flashing, and will certainly inquire the owner's name. Yet would I rather it had faced the evening sun, because more people are abroad at sunset than at dawn.'

'The morning sun is better for the growth of plants, and it comports the evening shadow, which is most agreeable,' murmured Suleymân, who stretched his length upon the ground before us, chewing a flower-stem with an air of wisdom.

As we were there conversing lazily, one of the peasant-partners in the land came through the trees, bringing a tray with cups of coffee, which he had prepared for our refreshment.

'The Lord preserve your hands, O Câsim,' sighed Suleymân. 'You come at the very moment when my soul said "coffee."'

The peasant Câsim beamed with pleasure at the thanks we showered on him, and, squatting down, inquired if we had yet decided anything.

'Aye,' I replied. *'In sh'Allah* we shall cut down these three olive trees and put the house instead of them.'

At that his smile gave place to grave concern.

He said: 'That may not be.'

'Why not?' I asked.

'Because we have no right to touch these trees.'

'But the *Sheykh* Ali told me that this terrace was his property.'

'That is so, as to the land. The trees are different.'

'To whom, then, do these trees belong?'

'To different people.'

'How can I know which trees are ours, which theirs?'

'Your Honour need not trouble. They are able to distinguish.'

'But they must walk upon our land to reach their trees!'

'Without a doubt.'

'But it is unheard of!'

'Perhaps; but it has been the way since Noah's flood.'

'If your Honour condescends to read the Bible he will notice that, in the bargain which our lord Abraham made for the cave of Machpelah, the trees upon the land are mentioned separately,' put in Suleymân, who had a well-stored mind.

I took no notice, but continued my alarmed inquiries.

'How many people own these trees?'

'Twenty or thirty.'

'And they trample on our land?'

'The case is so.'

'Who is their chief?'

'I know not; but the largest share, they say, is vested in Muhammad abu Hasan. His share of all the trees is twelve *kîrâts*, as much as all the others put together. They say so. Only Allah knows the truth!'

'I should like to speak to this Muhammad abu Hasan.'

'Upon my head; I go to fetch him,' answered Câsim, touching his brow in token of obedience.

When he was gone, Suleymân observed significantly:

'Have naught to do with all these fathers of *kîrâts*. When once the word "*kîrât*" is mentioned, flee the place, for you may be assured that it is the abode of all bedevilment. When once a man is father of but one or two *kîrâts*, he has the power of forty thousand for unreasoning annoyance.'

'And what, in mercy's name, is a *kîrât*?' I questioned.

'A *kîrât*,' replied Rashîd, as usual eager to explain, 'is that term into which all things visible and invisible are resolved and subdivided secretly, or may be subdivided at a person's pleasure. A *kîrât* is that which has no real existence unless a group of men agree together saying: "It is here or there." A *kîrât*——'

Suleymân cut short his explanation, saying simply: 'A *kîrât* is the twenty-fourth part of anything. If my soul is sick, I ask the doctor: "How many *kîrâts* of hope?" and according to his answer "four" or "twenty" I feel gladness or despair. To own but one *kîrât*, in this concern of property, is sometimes better than to own all the remaining three-and-twenty, as witness the affair of Johha, the greatest wiseacre this country has produced. Johha owned a house, consisting of a single room. Wishing to make a little money, he let his house to people for a yearly rent (which they paid in advance), reserving to himself the use of only

one *kîrât* of it. To show where his *kîrât* was situated Johha
drove a peg into the wall inside. After the tenants had been
in a week he brought a bag of beans and hung it on his
peg. No one objected; he was exercising his free right. A
few days later he removed the bag of beans and hung up
garlic in its place. Again a few days and he came with an
old cat which had been some time dead; and so on,
bringing ever more offensive things, until the tenants were
obliged to leave the house and forfeit their year's rent,
without redress, since Johha was within his rights.
Therefore I say to you, beware. These fathers of *kîrâts* will
spoil the property.'

Rashîd gave an appreciative chuckle, and was going to
relate some story of his own; but just then Câsim
reappeared, attended not by one man only but a score of
men—the owners of the trees, as it immediately appeared,
for they cried out, as they came up, that it would be a sin
for us to cut them down.

I asked them to elect a spokesman, as I could not deal
with all at once, and Muhammad abu Hasan was pushed
forward. He squatted, facing me, upon the ground, his men
behind him. The twigs and leaves of olives overhead
spread a filigree of moving shade upon their puckered
faces. They were evidently much perturbed in mind.

I asked them for how much they would consent to sell
those trees—showing the three I wished to fell to clear a
space for building.

'The freehold, meanest thou?' inquired their spokesman
anxiously. 'Not for five hundred pounds. But we would sell
a share.'

'I want no share. I want to cut them down.'

At that there was a general outcry that it must not be.

'The trees would remain yours until the end,' I told them, 'for I would let you have the wood for your own purposes, and, in addition, you would have a pretty sum of money.'

There ensued a long and whispered consultation before Muhammad abu Hasan answered me. At length he said:

'It may not be. Behold, we all are the descendants of one man who owned these trees in ancient days. But we are not brothers, nor yet uncles' children, and there is jealousy among us. We quarrel near to fighting every year about the produce of these trees, each man perceiving that he has been cheated of his proper share. But that is not so very serious, for each man hopes that next year he will get a larger share in compensation. Suppose, instead of trees which bear fruit every year, we had a sum of money. In that case the division would admit of no redress, and those who thought themselves defrauded would bear lifelong malice. Therefore I say: We will not have those trees cut down; but we are prepared, upon the other hand, to sell you all our trees upon this terrace if you, on your side, will assign to us but two *kîrâts* of all your trees, these trees included.'

'Allah destroy the dwelling of your two *kîrâts*,' I cried out angrily. 'I will have none of them. Nor will I make my dwelling in the neighbourhood of men so foolish. I shall seek elsewhere.'

The peasants chuckled at my curse on the *kîrâts*. They murmured an apology, but seemed relieved, as they went off.

Suleymân, who had to leave us on the following day, then gave me good advice.

He said: 'It is no use for you to deal with little people who wish to make the most of their small lands, who have mean, dirty houses. You have a friend among the great *sheykhs* of the *Drûz*. Go to him in his castle and explain your wish. He owns a score of noble houses which he does not use, and for the love of you he will not count the price too closely. Moreover, he will think that, showing favour to an Englishman, he will earn the good opinion of the British Government. He has political ambitions. All great men are fools or malefactors.'

'That is the best of counsel,' said Rashîd. And, having nothing else in mind, we acted on it.

BUYING A HOUSE

Even great men in the East rise early; so, when I arrived before the castle of the great *Druze* chief at six o'clock of a summer's morning, I was not surprised to find a crowd of black-cloaked and white-turbaned mountaineers already waiting for an audience of his grace; nor yet, when I had gained admittance as a favoured person, to find the chief himself afoot and wide awake. What did surprise me was to see him clad in *Stambûli* frock-coat and all its stiff accompaniments at an hour when even the most civilised of *Pashas* still wears native dress. He heard of my desire to settle in his country with surprise and seeming pleasure, and made me sit beside him on a sofa in an upper chamber of magnificent proportions—spoilt, to my taste, by gaudy Frankish furniture and certain oleographs of the crowned heads of Europe which adorned its walls.

He thought, as is the way of Orientals, visibly, with finger pressed to brow. Then he exclaimed:

'I have a house close by, across the glen—a little ruinous, perhaps, but we can soon repair it. Come to the window; you can see the place from here.' He pointed out a kind of thickset tower which crowned a pretty village set in orchards. 'If you care to see it we will go there when I have received my people.'

He invited me to go with him to the reception; but, having seen the crowd outside, I thought it wisdom to go back rather to the village *khan* where I had left my horse, to warn Rashîd to have things ready for a start, and get some breakfast.

I returned in two hours' time, to find the chief already mounted on a splendid charger, led by a no less splendid servant, setting forth in search of me, 'with half the world for tail,' as Rashîd put it.

It was in truth a long procession which meandered down the steep and rocky pathway, deep in the shade of walls and overhanging trees, to the ravine, forded the stream, and climbed the other bank.

The village, when we reached it, was in great commotion, all its people crowding to the wide *meydân*, or levelled ground for horsemanship, spread out before the house which might be mine. In the midst of this *meydân* there was a fine old carob tree, with a stone bench all round the foot of its enormous trunk.

The house itself was an old fortress, built of solid stone, with arrow slits as well as modern windows, and an arched doorway at the top of wide stone steps. Against it nestled lesser houses of the village which seemed to climb up towards it for protection.

Some men of consequence came forth to greet the chief, who then dismounted with their servile aid. He introduced me to a turbaned *Druze* of reverend appearance, who (he said) at present occupied the house, and also to the son of the said turbaned *Druze*, who knew a little French and longed to air it.

The turbaned one, whose name was *Sheykh* Huseyn, was called on to refresh his chieftain's memory with regard to various details of the house and property and all the feudal rights and privileges appertaining thereunto. He did so, as in duty bound, but in a very mournful tone.

His son explained: *Tu fiens habiter, nous defons quitter. Mon bère n'aime bas quitter. Très bon marché*—from which I guessed that they had occupied the house rent-free till they had come to look upon it as their own.

Leaving aside the land, which we should visit presently, the owner of the house, I was informed, had jurisdiction over the *meydân*, which was in times of peace the village square, and owned one-fifth part of the great tree in its midst. He also owned a fifth of all the water flowing or to flow from the great village spring; and had the right to call upon the *fellâhîn* for one day's work a year in return for his protection of their land from enemies. When I inquired by what means I could possibly secure my fifth share of the water from the spring, the chief informed me that the stipulation was in case the source diminished in dry seasons, which, thank the Lord, it never yet had done.

We viewed the house, and I was pleased with the great vaulted rooms, in which the pots and pans and bedding of the *Sheykh* Huseyn appeared like nothing, and the women of the family of *Sheykh* Huseyn, close-veiled against our inroad, made themselves exceeding small; and then, remounting, we went off to view the land. This was scattered all about the mountain side—a terrace here, a terrace there. It took us a long while to see the whole of it.

The chief, fatigued, alighted and sat down beneath some walnut trees. He ordered *Sheykh* Huseyn to cause refreshments to appear. The latter shouted, and a dozen villagers went tearing off. In a very little time a meal of honeyed cakes and fruit was set before us, and the ceremony of making coffee was in progress on a brazier near us in the shade.

'Allah! Allah!' sighed the *Sheykh* Huseyn, telling his beads.

'*Mon bère est triste, tu vois. Il aime bas quitter,*' murmured his hopeful son in tones of high delight, the feeling proper to express before a new acquaintance of my quality.

'Curse the religion of these flies! It is extremely hot!' exclaimed the chief in momentary irritation.

The trees went with the land without exception, I was glad to hear. One-fifth of all the produce of that land of any kind whatever would be mine, the rest belonging to the husbandmen by immemorial right. There was never such a thing as wages for the cultivation of the land.

The *Sheykh* Huseyn implored us to return to luncheon at his house, protesting that he had commanded a great feast to be prepared; but the chief declared we were too busy to allow ourselves that pleasure. As we were then some way below the village, we did not go back thither, but rode off along a path through orchards till we found the road to the ravine.

At taking leave, the eyes of *Sheykh* Huseyn met mine a moment. They were large, benevolent, brown eyes, and they expressed much inward sorrow, while on his lips there broke the smile demanded of politeness.

'Au refoir, mon cher! Au blaisir!' cried his hopeful son.

Rashîd came up behind me as we rode along, and poured into my ear a wondrous tale of how the *Sheykh* Huseyn was our ill-wisher and would do his best to make things lively for us if we took the place. He had conversed with people of the village while we viewed the house.

'But the majority are in our favour,' he assured me, with grave satisfaction. 'They do not love the *Sheykh* Huseyn, who is a miser and a hypocrite. They say, please God, we shall humiliate him to the very depth of shame.'

He spoke as if we were at war, and within sight of victory, as if we were already settled in the place. And I was glad, because it augured well for my content if I should buy the place, which I was now resolved to do if I could anyhow afford it.

'The price will be too great, I fear,' was my reply; whereat he sighed, observing that the place was of a nature to exalt our honour.

Returning to the castle of the chieftain, I was ushered to his private chamber, where I broached at once the burning question of the price. He said: 'God knows I wish to give you house and land since you desire them. But I have a mortgage on some other lands of mine which vexes me, because, though I can find the interest—which is exorbitant—each year, I cannot in this country lay my hands upon the principal. Discharge that debt for me and, God reward you , take the house and land.'

He named a sum of money. I could not believe my ears, it was so little as compared with what I judged to be the value of the property. It was well within the sum at my disposal. I wished to write a cheque out there and then; but he forbade me, saying: 'Allah knows I might mislay the paper or destroy it in a moment of forgetfulness. Do you in kindness pay my creditor and bring me the discharge.'

He named an Armenian gentleman of my acquaintance—an amiable, learned man of modest means, the last person in the country whom I should have thought a usurer. Nor was he one habitually, for he himself informed me that this loan to the *Druze* chieftain was his sole investment of the kind. I called on him one afternoon in the city, and handed him my cheque, explaining how the matter stood.

'You do me a bad turn. Unlucky day!' he sighed as he received it. 'My little fortune was more safe with him than in a bank, and every year it brought me in a pretty income. Where can I find another such investment.'

With groans he wrote out the receipt, which in due time I carried to the chief, who thanked me and assured me that the house was mine and should be made so formally.

I then rode over to the house again, and with Rashîd planned out the changes we desired to make, the *Sheykh* Huseyn following us about gloomily, and his cheerful son bestowing on us his advice in broken French. They knew their tenancy was at an end. The *Sheykh*, resigned at length to the inevitable, sought to establish good relations with me; and he also gave us counsel, which Rashîd, who viewed him as our deadly foe, at once rejected. Under these rebuffs the old man became quite obsequious.

His son exclaimed excitedly: '*Mon bère est heureux, tu vois. If feut bas quitter. Il feut rester afec toi comme chef de serfice.*'

A DISAPPOINTMENT

Considering that I had bought a house and land exactly to my taste, and likely, as Rashîd declared, to raise our honour in the country, I felt that I had earned the right to take a holiday. Whenever I have done anything decisive it is my instinct to withdraw myself a little from the scene of action and inure myself by contemplation to the new position of affairs. Accordingly, having surveyed the house and land as owner, I set off with Rashîd upon a ten days' journey beyond the reach of telegrams and letters.

At the end of the ten days we rode into Beyrout, and put up at a little hostelry, which we frequented, built out on piers above the sea. There I found two letters waiting for me, one from the great *Druze* chief who sold to me my house and land.

'Never,' he wrote, 'have I had to endure such disrespect and ignominy. It is not at all what I expected from your friendship. In obedience to the Consul's order, I wrote express to the *Khawâjah* ——, my creditor, informing him that there had been some error and entreating him to send your cheque in to the British Consulate. I hope to God you have received it safely before this. My health has suffered from this huge indignity. I shall not long survive this cruel shame.'

The second letter was from Her Britannic Majesty's Consul-General, enclosing my cheque written to the order of the Armenian gentleman for the amount of the mortgage which he held upon my *Druze* friend's property,

164

and adjuring me to pay a visit to the Consulate without delay.

I went that afternoon. The outer office was crowded with the usual set of English and would-be English persons who went there for gossip. My appearance called forth more or less derisive shouts. I was a nice young man to go and buy a village—from a native, too!—without the forethought to secure a title to the property! It was plain that they knew more about the matter than I did myself. I felt ashamed, and must have looked dejected, I suppose, for they changed their tone for one more genial, crying: 'Cheer up, man! We've all been through it. You know now what these devils really are. They'll always do you, if they can. It's no shame to you at your age. They're so devilish clever.'

I did not know then, nor do I know today, that I had ever been defrauded seriously, or deceived, by any native of the country, but the legend ran, and doubtless runs, to that effect.

Then I was called into the Consul's presence and strongly blamed by him for running off just at the moment when my presence was most needed. I had written joyously to tell him of my purchase. I now heard that I should have waited for his reply before concluding it. A man does not buy tracts of land like that, I was severely told. And as I was so very young and (he implied it) idiotic, he had intervened to stop the sale, pending inquiries and the discharge of certain formalities which were legally required. If the seller went into the court and had the transfer registered and a proper deed of sale made out, then well and good; but he understood that there was some objection on the seller's part. If not, then he advised me to give up the whole idea. Profoundly conscious of my youth, and mindful of past kindness on the Consul's part, I was, of course, impressed. I thought I had indeed been foolish, even mad; and promised to do all that he required of me. As I went through the outer office, looking more than ever downcast, I was hailed with further adjurations to cheer up, for they had all been through it.

Rashîd was more depressed than even I was when I told him of the sudden downfall of our hopes. He cursed the Consul and the *Druzes* indiscriminately. But on our journey up into the mountains his reconstructive mind transfigured my misfortunes, making of them an event well calculated to 'exalt our honour.' So great was my consideration in my native country that the Queen herself had written to the Consul-General to take care of me and see that I was not defrauded when I bought my land. The Consul, who had been neglectful of me, and knew nothing of the land I wished to buy, had been afraid of the Queen's anger, hence his mad activity. I did not hear that version at the time, nor from Rashîd's own lips; but it came to my ears eventually, after its vogue was past.

We both hoped, however, that the house and land would yet be ours.

I found the *Druze* chief prostrate with humiliation and bewilderment. He greeted me with monstrous sighs, and told me how ashamed he was, how very ill. His eyes reproached me. What had he ever done to me that I should loose upon him such a swarm of ignominies. I felt humiliated and ashamed before him, an honourable man who had been treated like a rogue on my account.

'I shall not survive these insults, well I know it. I shall die,' he kept lamenting. 'All my people know the way I have been treated—like a dog.'

I told him that there had been a misunderstanding, and

that the shame which he had suffered had been all my fault, because I had been absent for my selfish pleasure at the moment when I might have saved him by a simple statement of the facts.

'I shall not easily recover,' the chief groaned. 'And then that debt which I was so delighted to pay off is once again upon my shoulders.'

I explained then that the Consul's stopping of the sale was not conclusive, but provisional; his only stipulation being that, before I paid, all the legal formalities necessary to the transfer should have been fulfilled.

'He asks no more than that your Excellency will condescend to go before the *Caïmmacâm* with witnesses, and have a proper title-deed made out.'

At those words, uttered in all innocence, the great man shuddered violently and his face went green. I feared that he would have a fit, but he recovered gradually; and at last he said: 'It is a cruel thought, and one which must have been suggested to him by my enemies. Know that the *Caïmmacâm* at present is my rival and most deadly foe. We have not met on terms of speech for many years; our servants fight at chance encounters on the road. It is but five years since I held the post of Governor which he now occupies. When, by means of calumny and foul intrigue against me at Stamboul, he managed to supplant me, I swore a solemn oath that I would never recognise the Government nor seek its sanction so long as he remained its representative. And now the Consul bids me have recourse to him. By Allah, I would sooner be impaled alive.'

He paused a moment, swallowing his rage, then added:

'This, however, I will do. I will summon all the chiefs of all my people—every head of every family—hither to your presence and command them all to witness that the property is yours. I will make them swear to defend you and your successors in possession of it with their lives if need be, and to leave the obligation as a sacred charge to their descendants. That, I think, would be sufficient to assure you undisturbed possession if I die, as well I may, of this unheard-of treatment. And if I live till happier times—that is, to see the downfall of my enemy—then you shall have the Government certificate which the Consul deems of such immense importance.'

I now know that the kind of treaty which he thus proposed, laying a solemn charge on all his people—who would have been, of course, my neighbours—to defend my right, would have been worth a good deal more than any legal document in that wild country. The Armenian gentleman, who was delighted that his mortgage still held good, told me as much when next I saw him in the city. He thought me foolish not to jump at it, particularly when the land was offered to me for a song. But the Consul's prohibition, and the warnings of the English colony, possessed more weight with me just then than his opinion, or, indeed, my own, for I was very young.

I told the chieftain it was not enough.

'Then I am truly sorry,' he replied, with dignity; 'but there the matter ends. I have told your Honour the reason why I cannot go to court at present.'

Rashîd was sad when I informed him of my failure. Once more he cursed the *Druzes* and all Consuls. And as we rode back through the mountains he was wrapped in thought. He came at length to the conclusion that this, too, redounded to our honour, since anybody less exalted than ourselves would certainly have jumped at such an offer as the chief had made to me. But everything, for us, must be performed in the most perfect manner. We were tremendous sticklers for formality.

There was only one thing he could not get over.

'It is the triumph of our enemy, that *Sheykh* Huseyn,' he told me. 'I hate to think of him in comfort in our house.'

Concerning Crime & Punishment

If we wished to stay in any place for more than a day or two, Rashîd, upon arrival, wandered through the markets and inquired what dwellings were to let, while I sat down and waited in some coffee-house. Within an hour he would return with tidings of a decent lodging, whither we at once repaired with our belongings, stabling our horses at the nearest *khan*.

My servant was an expert in the art of borrowing, so much so that no sound of disputation on that subject reached my ears. It seemed as if the neighbours came, delighted, of their own accord to lend us pots and pans and other necessaries. He also did the cooking and the marketing without a hitch, giving a taste of home to the small whitewashed chamber, which we had rented for a week, it might be, or a month at most.

When obliged to go out upon any errand, Rashîd was always worried about leaving me alone, regarding me as careless of my property and so untrusty from the point of view of one who idolised it.

'If your Honour should be seized with a desire to smell the air when I am absent,' he would say, 'do not forget to lock the door and place the key in the appointed hiding-place where I can find it. There are wicked people in the world. And while you sit alone, keep our revolver handy.'

He told me that in cities robberies of private dwellings are oftener committed at high noon, when many houses are left empty, than at night, when they are full of snoring folk. I did not doubt the truth of this assertion, but differed from him in believing that we harboured nothing likely to attract a thief.

'I would not lose the buckle of a strap, a single grain of sesame, by such foul means,' he would reply with vehemence.

One morning—it was in Damascus—he went out, after imploring me as usual to take care of everything. The room we occupied was at the end of a blind alley, up a flight of nine stone steps. The alley led into a crowded, narrow street, bordered with shops of many-coloured wares, which at that point was partly shaded by a fine old ilex tree. From where I sprawled upon a bed of borrowed cushions in the room, reading a chap-book I had lately purchased—*The Rare Things of Abu Nawwâs*—I saw the colour and the movement of that street as at the far end of a dark kaleidoscope, for all the space between was in deep shadow.

When a man turned up our alley—a most rare occurrence—I noticed his appearance. It was rather strange. He wore an old blue shirt, and on his head a kind of turban, but of many colours and, unlike any I had ever seen upon the natives of the country, with an end or streamer hanging loose upon one side. In complexion, too, he was a good deal darker than a Syrian, and yet had nothing of the negro in his looks. Something furtive in his manner of approach amused me, as suggestive of the thief of Rashîd's nightmares. I moved into the darkest corner of the room and lay quite still. He climbed our steps and filled the doorway, looking in.

It happened that Rashîd had left a bag of lentils, bought that morning, just inside. The thief seized that and, thinking he was unobserved, was going to look round for other spoil, when I sat up and asked to know his business. He gave one jump, replied: 'It is no matter,' and was gone immediately. I watched him running till he vanished in the crowded street.

Rashîd returned. I told him what had happened in his absence, but he did not smile. He asked me gravely to describe the man's appearance, and, when I did so, groaned: 'It is a *Nûri* (gipsy). Who knows their lurking-places? Had it been a townsman or a villager I might perhaps have caught him and obtained redress.' He said this in a manner of soliloquy before he turned to me, and, with reproachful face, exclaimed:

'He stole our bag of lentils and you watched him steal it! You had at hand our good revolver, yet you did not shoot!'

'Why should I shoot a man for such a trifle?'

'It is not the dimensions or the value of the object stolen that your Honour ought to have considered, but the crime! The man who steals a bag of lentils thus deliberately is a wicked man, and when a man is wicked he deserves to die; and he expects it.'

I told him that the gipsy was quite welcome to the lentils, but he would not entertain that point of view. After trying vainly to convince me of my failure to perform a social duty, he went out to the establishment of a coffee-seller across the street, who kept his cups and brazier in the hollow trunk of the old ilex tree, and set stools for his customers beneath its shade, encroaching on the public street. Thither I followed after a few minutes, and found him telling everybody of the theft. Those idlers all agreed with him that it was right to shoot a thief.

'All for a bag of lentils!' I retorted loftily. 'God knows I do not grudge as much to any man.'

At that there rose a general cry of 'God forbid!' while one explained:

'It were a sin to refuse such a thing to a poor man in need who came and begged for it in Allah's name. But men who take by stealth or force are different. Think if your Honour had destroyed that thief, the rascal would not now be robbing poorer folk, less able to sustain the loss! Suppose that bag of lentils had been all you had! There may be people in the world as poor as that.'

'Why should I kill a man who offered me no violence?' I asked defiantly.

'Why should you not do so, when the man is evidently wicked?'

'Why do the Franks object to killing wicked people?' asked the coffee-seller with a laugh. 'Why do they nourish good and bad in their society?'

'It is because they are without religion,' muttered one man in his beard.

An elder of superior rank, who overheard, agreed with him, pronouncing in a tone of gentle pity:

'It is because they lose belief in Allah and the life to come. They deem this fleeting life the only one vouchsafed to man, and death the last and worst catastrophe that can befall him. When they have killed a man they think they have destroyed him quite; and, as each one of them fears such destruction for himself if it became the mode, they condemn killing in their laws and high assemblies. We, when we kill a person, know that it is not the end. Both killed and killer will be judged by One who knows the secrets of men's breasts. The killed is not deprived of every hope. For us, death is an incident: for them, the end. Moreover, they have no idea of sacrifice. Killing, with them, is always the result of hate.'

'What does your Honour mean by that last saying?' I inquired with warmth.

The old man smiled on me indulgently as he made answer sadly:

'Be not offended if we speak our mind before you. We should not do so if we wished you ill. Here, among us, it is not an unheard-of thing for men to kill the creatures they love best on earth; nor do men blame them when, by so doing, they have served the cause of God, which is the welfare of mankind. Thus it was of old the rule, approved of all the world, that every Sultan of the line of Othman had to kill his brothers lest they should rise against him and disturb the peace of all the realm. Was it not like depriving life of all its sweetness thus to destroy their youth's companions and their nearest kin? Yet, though their hearts were in the bodies of their victims, they achieved it. And the victims met their death with the like fortitude, all save a few of less heroic mould.

'Now, I have read some histories written by the Europeans. They do not understand these things at all. They think us merely cruel—just as we, in the same unperceiving manner, think them merely covetous. Yet I disagree with your good servant in the present case. I think that you were right to spare that *Nûri*.'

Rashîd, who, with the rest of the assembly, had listened to the old man's speech with reverence, exclaimed:

'It is not just this *Nûri* or that bag of lentils, O my lord! My master is thus careless always. He never locks the door when he goes out during my absence, though all that we possess is in that room.'

'Thy lord is young.' The old man smiled upon me kindly, and proceeded then to read me a mild lecture on my carelessness, detailing to me the precautions which he took himself, habitually, when shutting up his house or place of business, including pious formulas which he made me repeat after him. While he was thus instructing me, Rashîd went off, returning in about three minutes with a face of indignation strangely and incongruously mixed with triumph.

Taking his stand before me in the very middle of the seated crowd, he said:

'You left the door wide open even after you had seen that *Nûri* steal the bag of lentils. I have this minute been to look and I have seen. With our revolver lying in the full light of the doorway! Merciful Allah! What is to be done with you?'

The old man, my preceptor, laughed aloud; and at the sound Rashîd, whose desperation was not acted, wept real tears. The people round us tried in vain to comfort him.

THE UNWALLED VINEYARD

One morning, as we rode along, we came to vineyards on a valley-side. Rashîd dismounted and began to pick the grapes. Suleymân dismounted likewise, and invited me to do the same.

'But it is stealing,' I objected.

'Allah! Allah!' moaned Suleymân, as one past patience. He hung his head a moment, limp all over, as if the spirit had been taken out of him; then called out to Rashîd, who was devouring grapes:

'Return, O malefactor, O most wicked robber! you are guilty of a fearful crime. Thy master says so.'

Rashîd came back to us immediately, bringing a purple bunch, which he was going to give to me when Suleymân prevented him, exclaiming:

'Wouldst dishonour our good lord by placing in his hands the fruit of infamy, as if he were a vile accomplice of your crime? For shame, O sinful depredator, O defrauder of the poor!'

Rashîd gaped at him, and then looked at me. I held out my hand for the grapes.

'Touch them not, for they are stolen!' cried Suleymân.

'I know not what you would be at, O evil joker,' said Rashîd, with warmth; 'but if you call me a thief again, I'll break your head.'

'I call you thief? you are mistaken, O my soul! By Allah! I am but the mouthpiece of your master here, who says that to pluck grapes out of this vineyard is to steal.'

176

Rashîd looked towards me, half incredulous, and, seeing that I ate the grapes with gusto, answered with a laugh:

'He does not understand our customs, that is all. By Allah! there is no man in this land so churlish or so covetous as to begrudge to thirsty wayfarers a bunch of grapes out of his vineyard or figs or apricots from trees beside the road. To go into the middle of the vineyard and pick fruit there would be wrong, but to gather from the edge is quite allowable. If we were to come with sumpter-mules and load them with the grapes, that would be robbery; but who but the most miserly would blame us for picking for our own refreshment as we pass, anymore than he would stop the needy from gleaning in the fields when corn is cut. What your Honour thinks a crime, with us is reckoned as a kindness done and taken.'

'Aye,' said Suleymân, whose gift was for interpretations, 'and in the same way other matters which your Honour blames in us as faults are in reality but laudable and pious uses. Thus, it is customary here among us to allow the servant to help himself a little to his master's plenty in so far as food and means of living are concerned. The servant, being wholly given to his master's service, having no other means of living, still must live; aye, and support a wife and children if he have them; and it is the custom of our great ones to pay little wages, because they have but little ready money. Upon the other hand, they have possessions and wide influence, in which each servant is their partner to a small extent. No one among them would object to such small profits as that cook of yours, whom you condemned so fiercely, made while in your service. If the master does not care to let the servant gain beyond his wages, he must pay him wages high enough for his existence—certainly higher wages than you paid that cook.'

'I paid him what he asked,' I said indignantly.

'And he asked what he thought sufficient in consideration of the profits he felt sure of making in your service—a foreigner and a young man of many wants.'

'I had told him that you are of all men living the most generous!' put in Rashîd. My dismissal of that cook had long been rankling in his mind. 'It is the custom of the country,' he subjoined, defiantly.

'It is a custom which I very heartily dislike,' I answered. 'It seems to me that people here are always grasping. Look at the prices which the merchants ask, the way they bargain. They fight for each para as if it were their soul's salvation. They are mad for gain.'

'Again you are mistaken,' answered Suleymân. 'They do not ask too much from avarice, but for the sake of pastime. Indeed, you will find sometimes that the price they ask is less than the real value of the object, and still they let the buyer beat it down—for mere amusement of the argument and for the sake of seeing what devices he will use. In addition, they will give the buyer a nice cup of coffee—sometimes two cups of coffee if the argument is long—and as many glasses full of sherbet as he cares to drink.'

'And if the buyer will not pay the price, though much reduced, the merchant often will present the object to him, as happened to your Honour in Aleppo only the other day,' put in Rashîd.

'That was only a device to shame me into buying it.'

'No, by your Honour's leave!'

'Rashîd may well be right,' said Suleymân, 'although I cannot judge of the peculiar instance since I was not present.'

Just then we came around a shoulder of the hill, and saw

some people, men and women, harvesting the grapes in a much larger vineyard.

'Now you shall see!' exclaimed Rashîd exultantly. He got down off his horse and stooped over the nearest vines. The workers, seeing him, set up a shout of *'Itfaddalû!'* (perform a kindness), the usual form of hospitable invitation. Since we refused to join them in the middle of the vineyard a man came wading towards us, bearing on his head a basket tray piled up with grapes. Suleymân picked out three monstrous clusters, one for each of us, with blessings on the giver. To my offer of payment the *fellâh* opposed a serious refusal, saying: 'It would be a shame for me.'

'You see now!' said Rashîd, as we resumed our way. 'It is not robbery for wayfarers to take refreshment.'

'And as for the custom of the merchants,' added Suleymân, 'in asking a much higher price than that which they at last accept, what would you have? Those merchants are rich men, who have enough for all their needs. Their aim is not that of the Frankish traders: to increase their wealth by all means and outdistance rivals. Their object is to pass the time agreeably and, to that end, detain the customer as long as possible, the more so if he be a person like your Honour, who loves jokes and laughter. The greatest disappointment to our merchants is for the customer to pay the price first asked and so depart immediately. I have a rare thing in my memory which hits the case.

'Everyone has heard of Abdu, the great Egyptian singer, who died recently. His only daughter met her death in a distressing way. It was her wedding night, and bride and bridegroom died of suffocation owing to the scent of flowers and perfumes in the bedroom where they lay. At sight of the two corpses Abdu broke his lute and swore a solemn oath never to sing again.

'He was rich—for he had earned much by his singing, often as much as a hundred pounds a night—and he sought some means to pass the time till death should come for him. He took a shop in Cairo, and hoped for pleasant conversation in the course of bargaining. But the Egyptians wished to hear him sing again, and men of wealth among them planned together to buy up his whole stock-in-trade immediately. This happened thrice, to the despair of Abdu, who saw his hope of pastime taken from him. In the end he was compelled to get the *Câdi* to release him from his vow, and sing again, although he would have much preferred to be a merchant. That shows the difference between a trader in our cities and one in any city of the Franks, whose sole desire is to sell quickly and repeatedly.'

'There is no accounting for tastes,' was my reply. 'For my part I detest this bargaining.'

'When that is understood by decent merchants they will not afflict you . They will ask you a fair price and let you go—though with regret, for they would rather spend an hour in talk with you ,' said Suleymân indulgently. 'It is a game of wits which most men like.' He shrugged his shoulders.

'Your Honour was relating yesterday,' observed Rashîd, with grievance in his tone, 'how an Englishman of your acquaintance in our country accused his servants of dishonesty. Doubtless he distrusted them and locked things up, which is the same as saying to them: "It is my locks and my vigilance against your wits." Few men of spirit could resist a challenge such as that, which is indeed to urge men on to robbery. But where the master trusts his servants and leaves all things to their care, only a son of infamy would dream of robbing him.'

'Let me propound the matter otherwise for understanding. Seeing that open vineyard, with a wall but two stones high, no man would think of plundering the crop of grapes. But surround that vineyard with a high, strong wall, and every son of Adam will conceive the project of clearing it of every cluster.'

'I should never think of such a thing.'

'That is because your Honour is accustomed to restraints and barriers,' said Suleymân. 'We, in the Sultan's dominions, have more freedom, praise to Allah! For us a high wall is an insult, save in cities.'

THE ATHEIST

Though I had known Suleymân for nearly two years, and
had had him with me for some six months of that time, I
had never seen him in his function of a dragoman, by
which he earned enough in two months of the year to keep
a wife and children in a village of the coasts of Tyre and
Sidon, of which he spoke with heart-moving affection,
though he seldom went there. It was only after much
insistence that he allowed us to conduct him thither on one
memorable occasion, when I could not but admire his
perfect manners as a despot. When first I met him he had
been a gentleman at large, and it was as that, and a familiar
friend, that he repaired to me whenever he had nothing
else to do. Judging from his gifts of conversation, which we
all admired, and his unbounded knowledge of the country,
I thought that, as a guide for tourists, he would be
invaluable. So, when I heard that English friends of mine
were coming out to Palestine, I wrote advising them to ask
for him, him only; and I was glad to hear soon afterwards
that he was with them. When they came north, I joined the
party at Damascus and travelled with them for their last
fortnight.

It did not take me many minutes in the camp to see that
Suleymân was not himself, and that my friends were not so
charmed with him as I had thought they would be. On the
first evening in their tent I heard complaints. They told me
he was most unconscionably lazy, and would not take them
to the places they desired to visit. The trouble was, as I
soon learnt, that they possessed a map and guidebook

which they studied reverently every night, finding out places said therein to be of interest. Suleymân, on his side, had, at setting out, possessed a plan to make their tour the most delightful one imaginable. He hoped by visiting selected spots and people to give it sequence and significance. In a word, he was an artist in travel, wishing to provide them with delicious memories, while they were English and omnivorous of facts and scenes. When he learnt from various rebuffs that they would not confide themselves to him, he lost all pleasure in the tour. It was a listless and disgusted upper servant, most unlike the man I knew, whom I found in gorgeous raiment sitting by the cook's fire in the gardens of Damascus, which were then a wilderness of roses.

He did not explain matters to me all at once. When I reproached him for neglecting friends of mine, he answered only: 'It is the will of Allah, who made men of different kinds, some sweet, some loathsome.' But my arrival mended things a little. At least, my English friends professed to see a great improvement in the conduct of Suleymân and all the servants. I think it was because the poor souls knew that they had someone now to whom they could express their grievances, someone who would condescend to talk with them; for nothing is more foreign to the Oriental scheme of life than the distance at which English people keep their servants. In the democratic East all men are equal, as far as rights of conversation are concerned. It is a hardship for the Oriental to serve Europeans, and only the much higher and more certain wages bring him to it.

My English friends had few good words to say for any of their Arab servants; but I found they had conceived a perfect hatred for the cook, who had undoubtedly a villainous appearance. He was a one-eyed man with a strong cast in his surviving eye. A skull-cap, which had once been white, concealed his shaven poll, and his long pointed ears stood out upon it. He wore a shirt of indigo impaired by time, over which, when riding, he would throw an ancient Frankish coat, or, if it chanced to rain, a piece of sacking. His legs were bare, and he wore scarlet slippers. To see him riding on an ass hung round with cooking tins, at the head of the procession of the beasts of burden, suggested to the uninformed spectator that those beasts of burden and their loads had all been stolen.

I spoke about him to Suleymân one day when in my company he had regained his wonted spirits, telling him of the extreme dislike my friends had taken to the man.

'They are foolish,' he replied, 'to grumble at the figure of a mill which grinds good flour. They profit by his cooking, which is excellent. Indeed, he is the best cook in the world, and most particular. I took great trouble to secure him for this expedition, knowing that the *Khawâjât* were friends of yours.' The tone of grievance in his voice became acute.

I feared that he was going to cry, so answered quickly:

'It is not that. They like his cooking. But his manners——'

'What know they of his manners? Has he ever entered the saloon or bed-tent to defile them? Has he ever spoken insult in their hearing? Inform me of his crime, and I will beat him bloody. But well I know he has done nothing wrong, for I have kept him in the strictest order all these days. It is only his appearance they object to; and that is God's affair, not theirs. The Lord repay them!'

'You say that you have kept him in strict order? Is that necessary?'

'Of course it is, for the poor man is mad. I thought his

madness would amuse them; it is very funny. But Allah knows that there is not a laugh in all their bodies. So I have kept him from approaching them.'

The word '*majnûn*,' which I have here translated 'mad,' has often, as I knew, a complimentary value; and I gathered from Suleymân's way of speaking that the cook was not a raving maniac, but rather what in English country-places we should call 'a character.'

I cultivated his acquaintance after that, and was astonished by his powers of story-telling and of mimicry; still more, perhaps, by a curious, dry scepticism, expressed facetiously and sometimes with profanity, which was evident in almost everything he said. This it was which chiefly pleased the waiter and the muleteers, who were his usual listeners, since they were together on the road. They would laugh and curse him in religious terms for a blasphemer and a wicked atheist, reproofs which he received as high applause. It was his custom to salute his friends with insults, which they took kindly from him, being what he was. They told me in low tones of awe, yet with a chuckle, that he had even sold his father's grave in a facetious way. But I could never get them to relate that story clearly.

I could understand then why Suleymân had kept him in strict order on the journey; for my English friends were quite incapable of seeing any fun in such a character. Nor did I ever tell them of the great adventure of that journey, in which their cook was very nearly done to death.

It happened near the village of Mejdel esh-Shems, down in the valley underneath Mount Hermon. We remained in camp there over Sunday, and on Sunday afternoon my friends were resting in their tent. Suleymân and I had seized that opportunity to go off for a ramble by ourselves, which did us good. We were returning to the camp in time for tea, when a crowd of *fellâhîn* came hurrying from the direction of our tents, waving their arms and shouting, seeming very angry. Suleymân called out to them to learn the matter.

'*Zandîq!*' (an atheist) they cried. '*Zandîq! Zandîq!*'

'Where?' I asked, eagerly.

'There, in yonder tent,' an old white-bearded man informed me, with wide eyes of horror. He pointed to the canvas windscreen against which our famous cook sat gazing at the kettle he had set to boil for tea. 'We go to fetch the wherewithal to kill him properly.'

'Stop!' said Suleymân peremptorily. 'You are mistaken. That is our cook—a good, religious man, but mad occasionally.'

'No, there is no mistake, O lords of honour,' cried a score of voices; while the old man who had pointed out the cook to me, explained:

'He said—may God protect us from the blame of it!—He said: "You see that mountain! It is I who made it. Prostrate yourselves before me for I made the world." We had been standing round him inoffensively, asking him questions, as the custom is, about his parentage, his trade, and so forth. But when we heard that awful blasphemy we rent our clothes, and ran in haste to fetch our weapons, as you see. Delay us not, for he must surely die.'

'Commit not such a wickedness! The man is mad.'

'No; he is sane.'

'Quite mad, I do assure you. Return with us, and I will prove it to your understanding,' cried Suleymân.

I added my assurance. They came back with us, but

murmuring, and in two minds. I could not but admire the simple piety which prompted them at once to kill a man whose speech betrayed him as an atheist. But I was very much afraid of what might happen, and of the sad impression it would make upon my English friends. And everything depended on the cook's behaviour.

'I tell you he is mad,' said Suleymân, advancing towards the fire. 'It were a sin for you to slay a fellow-creature thus afflicted. Come hither, *O Mansûr*,' he cried as to a dog.

The cook rose up and came towards us with a foolish air.

'Lie down before my horse. I would ride over you .'

The cook fell prostrate, then turned over on his back. His mouth hung open idiotically; his tongue lolled out.

'Now rise and kiss my boot.'

The cook obeyed. By that time there were murmurs of compassion from the would-be slayers.

'Spake I not truly?' asked Suleymân.

'Aye, O sun of verity! He is quite mad, the poor one,' said the old man who had acted spokesman. 'It were a sin for us to kill him, being in that state. His manner at the first deceived us. Allah heal him! How came the dreadful malady upon him?'

'It came upon him through the pangs of unrequited love.'

'Alas, the poor one! Ah, the misery of men! May Allah heal him!' cried the women, as the group of villagers moved off, contented. Just when the last of them passed out of sight the longest tongue I ever saw in man emerged from the cook's mouth, and the rascal put his finger to his nose in a derisive gesture. Those portents were succeeded by a realistic cock-crow.

'What makes the cook like that, devoid of reverence?' I asked of Suleymân.

'It is because he was born in Jerusalem,' was the astonishing reply. 'He is a Christian, and was born poor; and the quarrels of the missionaries over him, each striving to obtain his patronage for some absurd belief, have made him what he is—a kind of atheist.'

Selîm, the waiter, who was near and overheard this ending, burst out laughing.

'An atheist!' he cried. 'Your Honour understands? It means a man who thinks there is no God. Just like a beetle!' and he held his quaking sides.

Both he and Suleymân appeared to think that atheism was a subject to make angels laugh. And yet they were as staunch believers as those *fellâhîn*.

THE SELLING OF OUR GUN

I had been ill with typhoid fever. Just before my illness, the son of a *sheykh* in our neighbourhood had asked me to lend him my gun for a few days, since I never used it. There was nothing really which I cared to shoot. The village people rushed out in pursuit of every little bird whose tweet was heard, however distant, in the olive groves or up the mountain side. Jackals there were besides, and an occasional hyæna; and, in the higher mountains, tigers, so the people still persisted in declaring, meaning leopards, I suppose, or lynxes; for ignorant Arabs lump together a whole genus under one specific name, in the same way that they call all wild plants, which have neither scent nor market-value, grass. It was after we had sought those tigers vainly that I put away my gun.

The *sheykh's* son asked me for the loan of it, and I consented in the absence of Rashîd; who, when he heard what I had done, defiled his face with dust and wailed aloud. Suleymân, who happened to be with us at the moment, also blamed me, looking as black as if I had committed some unheard-of sin. It is unlucky for a man to lend his gun to anybody, even to the greatest friend he has on earth, they told me sadly; and that for no superstitious reason, but because, according to the law, if murder be committed with that weapon, the owner of the gun will be considered guilty no matter by whose hand the shot was fired.

'How do they know the owner of the gun?' I answered, scoffing.

'For every gun there is a *tezkereh* (license),' answered Rashîd; 'and he who holds the *tezkereh* is held responsible for every use to which that gun is put.'

It was, in fact, a rough-and-ready way of saying that the gun licence was not transferable. I remarked with satisfaction that I had no *tezkereh*, but that did not appear to reassure them in the least. They still were of opinion harm might come of it.

Then I fell ill and knew no more of daily life until I found myself in a hospital of the German Knights of St. John of Jerusalem, where the good sisters nursed me back to health.

Among the Arab visitors from far and near who came to see me as I lay in bed, was the youth who had borrowed my gun, together with his father and his brethren, who wept real tears and prayed for my complete recovery, talking as if they were beholden to me in some signal way. Their manner puzzled me a little at the time; but I had quite forgotten that perplexity when, discharged at last from hospital, I travelled back into the mountains with Rashîd.

On the very day of my return I got an invitation from that young man's father to dine with him at noon upon the morrow. Rashîd made a grimace at hearing of it and, when I asked him why, looked down his nose and said:

'He has our gun.'

'Aye, to be sure, and so he has!' I said. 'Tomorrow I must not forget to ask him for it.'

Rashîd looked big with tidings, but restrained himself and merely growled:

'You will not ask for it. I know your Honour! Nor will that rogue return it of his own accord.'

At the *sheykh*'s house next day I found a largeish company assembled in my honour, as it seemed. Innumerable were the compliments on my recovery, the pretty speeches and remarks, to which I made reply as best I could. The meal consisted of some thirty courses, and was set on trays upon the floor in the old, country fashion, everybody eating with his fingers from the dish. When it drew near an end, the son of the house glanced at his father meaningly, and getting in return a nod, rose up and left the room. He soon came back, carrying my gun, which he brought first to me as if for benediction, then handed round for the inspection of the other guests. There were cries of '*Ma sh'Allah!*' while they all praised its workmanship, one man opining that it must have cost a mint of money, another wishing he possessed its brother, and so forth. These exclamations and asides were evidently aimed at me, and it was somehow carried to my understanding that this exhibition of the gun, and not the public joy on my recovery, was the true reason of the feast and all attending it; though why it should be so I could not think.

'One thing that is remarkable about this gun,' explained the master of the house, 'is that it cannot miss the object aimed at. We have tried it at a target nailed upon a tree—I and my sons—at fifty and a hundred paces—aye, and more! And, by the Lord, the bullet always strikes exactly on the spot at which the gun is pointed, even though that spot be not much bigger than a gnat.'

And then, quite unaccountably, the whole assembly rose and tried to kiss my hands, as if the virtues of my gun were due to me. It was obviously not the moment to reclaim the weapon.

When I got home after that strange ovation, Rashîd received me coldly and observed:

'You do not bring our gun! You feared to ask for it! Did not I know how it would be? Oh, Allah, Allah!'

'I had no opportunity,' I told him; 'but I am going now to write and ask him to return it. Be ready for the letter. You will have to take it.'

'Upon my head and eye, with all alacrity,' Rashîd replied. 'Never did I rejoice so much in any errand. That rascal has been telling everybody that it is your gift to him, and boasting of his gun through all the mountains. No doubt, he counts upon your illness having dimmed remembrance, and hopes that you yourself may be deluded into thinking that it was a gift and not a loan.'

'Why did you not tell me this before?' I asked.

'Was it my business, till the question rose?'

I wrote a civil note to the young man, asking him to let me have the gun in a few days, as I was collecting my belongings for the journey back to England. I thanked him for the care which he had taken of my property, which was much better kept than when I lent it to him, as I had remarked that day. Rashîd received the missive and went off exulting.

Within an hour that young man came to me, without the gun, and in a state of most profound affliction and despair. Having shut the door with great precaution to make sure we were alone, he fell upon the ground and burst out crying, confessing that his passion for the gun had made him dream that it was his each night as he lay thinking ere he fell asleep.

'But I did not tell a soul that it was mine—did but dream it—until I knew your Honour was abed and like to die,' he told me naively, as something which might make his fault seem natural. 'I thought that you would die and leave it with me.'

So, thinking me as good as dead, he had told his father and his brothers that it was a gift from me, or, as it were, a legacy; and now the fame of my munificence, my love for him, had gone abroad. An hour ago, when he received my letter, he had confessed the truth at last and privately to his beloved father, who, while strongly blaming him for his deceit, was willing to pay any price I chose to put upon the weapon to save him from the horrid scandal of exposure. If the story became public in the country he would die of grief. The honour of a noble house was at my mercy.

The gun, so much admired, was quite a cheap one in reality. I had bought it for ten pounds three years before, in London, on the advice of an uncle skilled in all such matters. After a moment's thought, I said: 'Eight English pounds.'

Never in my life before or since have I beheld such transports of relief and gratitude, nor heard such heartfelt praises of my generosity. He told the money out before me there and then, insisted on embracing me repeatedly, and then rushed out, intent to tell his father.

When he had gone, Rashîd appeared before me, stern and aloof as the Recording Angel.

'It is a crime you have committed,' he exclaimed indignantly. 'That rascal told me as we came along together that his father was prepared to pay a hundred pounds to save their honour. He had sinned; it is but right his house should bear the punishment.'

'You would have done as I have done, in my position,' I assured him, laughing.

'In the position of your Honour,' was the dignified reply, 'I should either have made him pay a hundred pounds for our gun, or else persuaded him that it was worth a hundred pounds, and then presented it. In either case I should have crushed those people utterly. But, for a man in your position to accept eight pounds for such a weapon—and proclaim it worth no more—that is a shame! If your desire was money, you should not have touched the matter personally, but have left it altogether in the hands of me, your servant, who am always careful of your honour, which is mine as well.'

He sulked with me thereafter for two days.

MY BENEFACTOR

When I knew at length that I was going to leave Syria, I was seized with a desire to buy all kinds of notions of the country to show to my people at home—a very foolish way of spending money, I am now aware, for such things lose significance when taken from their proper setting.

In after days, when leaving Syria for England, the one thing I would purchase for myself was a supply of reed pens for Arabic writing. But on that first occasion I wished to carry the whole country with me.

There was an old, learned Christian of Beyrout, who had given me lessons in Arabic at various times, and always waited on me honourably whenever I alighted in that loveliest and most detestable of seaport towns. He wore the baggiest of baggy trousers, looking just like petticoats, a short fez with enormous hanging tassel, a black alpaca coat of French design, a crimson vest, white cotton stockings, and elastic-sided boots, convenient to pull off ere entering a room. He always carried in the street a silver-headed cane, which he would lean with care against the wall of any room he chanced to enter, never laying it upon the ground, or on a chair or table. In all the time of my acquaintance with him I never, that I can remember, saw him really smile, though something like a twinkle would occasionally touch his eyes beneath great bushy eyebrows, between black and grey. An extraordinarily strong and heavy grey moustache, with drooping ends, gave him a half-pathetic, half-imposing likeness to some aged walrus; so that some of the common people actually called him

'*Sheykh el Bahr*' (the old man of the sea)—which is the proper Arabic designation of a walrus.

He came to see me after I had left the hospital and was staying with some English friends for a few days before returning to the wilds for a farewell; and repeatedly praised Allah for my safe recovery. There never was a man more thoroughly respectable, more perfectly correct in every word and movement. He disapproved of poor Rashîd as a companion for me, because the latter dealt in vulgar language; and I feel certain that he would have disapproved of Suleymân, if he had ever seen that Sun of Wisdom in my company, for pandering to my desire for foolish stories. He was known as the *Mu'allim Costantîn*, a worthy man.

With his usual ceremonious salutation, suggestive of his high position as a representative of learning, he placed himself at my command for any purchases I wished to make; knowing, he said, that I was likely to be busy in the weeks before departure. And his offer was extremely welcome to me at the time. I wished, as I have said already, to buy lots of things; among others—why, I cannot now imagine—the whole costume of natives of the country. The *Mu'allim Costantîn* praised my intention, gravely declaring that it could not fail to interest my honoured relatives and lovers, and enlarge their minds, to know the details of a dress the most becoming in the world. In order that a full idea of Syrian raiment might be given, two suits and two long garments (corresponding to two other suits) were necessary, he pronounced. These, with the various articles of clothing which I then possessed and had grown used to wearing in the country, would be sufficient for the purposes of exhibition.

Upon the following day, as I was dressing, about ten o'clock (for I was still to some extent an invalid), there came a light knock at the door, and the *Mu'allim Costantîn* appeared, ushering in a friend of his, who was a tailor—a man as grave and worthy as himself, who there and then proceeded to take measurements, praising the proportions with which nature had endowed me, and asking Allah to fill out those parts which now were lean through illness. The moment of a man's uprising is—or was at that time, for old customs are now dying out—the one which servants, tradesmen, pedlars, and all who wished to ask a favour chose for visiting. On the morning after my arrival in an Eastern city where I happened to be known I have had as many as twelve persons squatting round upon the floor, watching a barber shave me, while a little boy, the barber's 'prentice, bearing towels, jug, and basin, waited upon him like an acolyte.

The tailor, having made the necessary notes, withdrew with many compliments. The *Mu'allim Costantîn* remained behind a moment, to assure me, in a loud stage-whisper, that the said tailor was a man whom I could trust to do the best for me, and that I might think myself extremely fortunate to have secured his services, as, being much sought after by the fashionables, he generally had more work than he could really do; but that, having taken, as he said, a fancy to me, he would certainly turn out a set of garments to enslave the heart. Having said this in the finest classic phraseology, he went out to rejoin the tailor in the passage; nor did I see him anymore until the very day of my departure, when, at the English Consul-General's hospitable house, I was waiting for the carriage which would take me to the quay.

I was told that someone wished to see me upon urgent business, and, going to the great *Liwân* or entrance-hall, I found my friend, his silver-headed cane leaned carefully against the wall as usual. He carried underneath his arm a number of large books. These he presented to me with a solemn bow.

'It occurred to me,' he said, 'that as your Honour has a predilection for all those curious and often foolish tales which circulate among the common people, you might not perhaps disdain these four poor volumes which I chance to have in my possession. Deign to accept them as a parting gift from me.'

I thanked him kindly, though in truth I was embarrassed, not knowing where to stow the books, since all my things were packed. And then he handed me the tailor's bill, which, with the clothes which I had ordered, had escaped my memory.

'Where are the clothes?' I asked, 'I had forgotten them.'

He pointed to a bundle pinned up honourably in a silken wrapper, reposing on the floor hard by the silver-handled cane. I tore the envelope and opened out the bill. It came to twenty pounds.

And I had got my money ready for my journey. I was going to visit some of the Greek Islands, Smyrna, and Constantinople, on my way to England, and had hoped, besides, to see a little of the Balkan States. To pay out twenty pounds was to reduce that journey by at least a fortnight. And, as I said, I had forgotten all about the clothes, regarding all my Syrian debts as fully paid.

The hall was empty; we were quite alone. I fear I stormed at the *Mu'allim Costantîn*, reminding him that he had promised that the clothes should not be dear.

'But,' he persisted, 'they are very cheap for the materials. If your Honour's wish was to pay less, you ought not to have chosen fabrics three parts silk. I did not know that you were counting money.'

He was right. Throughout my stay in Syria, until that moment, I had never counted money. Compared with

England, living in the country was absurdly cheap, and on my small allowance I had lived at ease. He might quite reasonably have supposed me to be very wealthy. But I was not in reasonable mood just then. I paid the bill, but in an angry manner; and while I was still talking to him, the *Cawwâs* arrived, and, close upon his heels, Rashîd in tears, to tell me that the carriage was in waiting. The grief I felt at leaving Syria, at parting from Rashîd and our Sheytân and many friends took hold of me. Hurriedly I said goodbye to the *Mu'allim Costantîn*, and I am glad to say I changed my tone at that last moment, and had the grace to bid him think no more of the whole matter. But I shall carry to my grave the recollection of his face of horror while I scolded, the look that told his grief that he had been deceived in me.

I went and shoved the books into my luggage here and there, gave Rashîd orders to send on the clothes, took leave of my kind hosts, and drove down in a hurry to the quay. It was not till some time after I arrived in England that I realised that the volumes which he had presented to me were a complete Bûlâc Edition of the *Thousand and One Nights*—a valuable book—which is my greatest treasure.

Nor have I ever had the chance of thanking the giver in a manner worthy of the gift, and wiping out the bad impression left by my ill-temper, for a letter which I wrote from England never reached him I am told, and when I next was in his country the *Mu'allim Costantîn* had gone where kindness, patience, courtesy, and all his other virtues are, I hope, rewarded.

Ω

Lightning Source UK Ltd.
Milton Keynes UK
UKOW03f0814250417
299834UK00004B/65/P